The Church Business Meeting

Elizabeth
Ferguson

The Church
Business Meeting

R. Dale Merrill

Judson Press ® Valley Forge

The Church Business Meeting
Copyright © 1968
Judson Press
Valley Forge, PA 19482-0851

Revised 1994

Permission is gratefully acknowledged to use quotations from the following books on parliamentary procedure:

Henry M. Robert, *Robert's Rules of Order, Revised* (Chicago: Scott, Foresman & Company, 1951). Copyright 1951 by Isabel H. Robert, used by permission.

George Demeter, *Demeter's Manual of Parliamentary Law and Procedure* (Boston: Bostonia Press, 1961).

Marguerite Grumme, *Basic Principles of Parliamentary Law and Protocol* (Westwood, N.J.: Fleming H. Revell Co., 1955).

Library of Congress Catalog Card NO. 68-28075

Printed in the U.S.A.

15 14 13 12 11 10 9
08 07 06 05 04 03 02 01 00

Foreword

Many books and tabulated charts have been prepared by competent authorities in the field of parliamentary procedure. Some are for broad and general usage, and others are designed for specific situations in recognition of differing purposes or responsibilities. Few, if any, publications of this character have been designed explicitly for the use and guidance of church groups. This book is so designed.

The author of this book is uniquely qualified to write with understanding authority. He is fully prepared in the field of law and has made the subject of parliamentary procedure a matter of study for years. He is an ordained minister with experience in the local church and in various types and sizes of councils and assemblies. The material contained herein has the double value of accuracy and appropriateness.

All too often church groups, whether in the relative simplicity of the local congregation or in the larger and more diverse variety of assemblages, assume that a reasonable meeting of the minds in the fellowship of a churchly setting provides an adequate basis for orderly procedure. This is not necessarily true. In fact, in most situations it is not true.

Most church groups meet for the purpose of making a decision that has a greater or lesser degree of legal significance. Churches and religious groups have corporate structures that in many settings conform with specific requirements of legal authority. It is important that the decision of the group be reached in an orderly manner, with full regard for the rights and privileges of each person in attendance, and in such form that an accurate and authoritative record may be perpetuated. Much confusion and many personal tensions can be eliminated by the observance of relatively simple procedures for church meetings.

This book is commended to all who have responsibility for the guidance of church groups, large or small, that they may achieve the orderly accomplishment of their corporate purposes.

William H. Rhoades

Contents

Purpose and Pattern   1

1. How Does God Speak to a Congregation?   5

2. Overcoming Difficult Situations   15

3. The Quorum, Order of Business,
   Reports, Resignations   41

4. Handling Amendments   49

5. Resolving Complex Issues   55

6. Nominations and Elections   73

7. Boards and Committees   81

8. Conventions, State and
   National Assemblies   95

   Bibliography   111

   Index   113

Additional Resources
Published by Judson Press
(1-800-458-3766)

The Church Newsletter Handbook
Clayton A. Lord Jr.

Church Officers at Work, Revised Edition
Glenn H. Asquith

Work of the Church: Getting the Job Done in Boards and Committees
David R. Sawyer

The Work of the Church Treasurer, Revised
Thomas E. McLeod

The Work of the Church Trustee
Orlando L. Tibbetts

The Work of the Clerk, New Edition
M. Ingrid Dvirnak

The Work of the Deacon and Deaconess
Harold Nichols

Work of the Pastoral Relations Committee
Emmett V. Johnson

The Work of the Sunday School Superintendent
Idris W. Jones, Revised by Ruth L. Spencer

The Work of the Usher
Alvin D. Johnson

The Work of the Worship Committee
Linda Bonn

Purpose and Pattern

This book is concerned with the reasons behind correct parliamentary procedure. When these are understood, the rules will drop into place and their reasonableness will become apparent. While the book deals primarily with church business meeting situations, the last chapter discusses particular procedures for state and national meetings of church bodies. All decision-making groups within the church structure, whether they are called boards, committees, societies, or whatever, will find the subject matter to be applicable. The book is general in scope so that all denominational groups may find help from the techniques suggested.

Although it is usual for church groups to function in an informal manner, it is important to know the rules. This book clearly stresses the idea that informality must take place within the limits of correct procedure. Church decision-making bodies should use the rules of order as tools to reach a consensus. The rules of order were never intended to become a straitjacket. Instead, they are the time-proven procedures for assisting a group to express its purpose.

This book has been written to help the members and leaders of church congregations overcome the common mistakes in parliamentary procedure that create problems in their business meetings. Consequently, those phases of parliamentary law that seldom come up in church-group meetings have not been handled in this book. Also, there is no attempt to deal with the order and arrangement of motions, although there is a chart on the last page of the book showing this relationship.

Because parliamentary law is concerned with the rights of persons as they function in groups, education in parliamentary law is education in good citizenship. There is no place where teaching opportunities are as open for this as in the church, nor is there any place where such teaching opportunities are so thoroughly neglected or thrown aside as in the church. Many other organizations, such as the P.T.A., women's clubs, and civic groups, offer courses in parliamentary procedure, knowing that concomitant with this knowledge comes better and more responsible leadership and citizenship.

In order that churches may better use their teaching opportunities, this book has been written so that a chapter, or a major subdivision of a chapter, may be read and discussed at the opening of each business meeting. By so doing, the full scope of parliamentary procedure for church groups can be covered in less than a year. (Another useful book for this purpose is *Demeter's Manual on Parliamentary Law and Procedure.*) If this is done regularly the group will grow in knowledge, and the business meeting will be turned into a wholesome time of Christian decision-making.

R. Dale Merrill

1

How Does God Speak to a Congregation?

How does God provide direction to a church congregation, board, or committee as the members seek to conduct their business? To be sure, meetings are customarily opened with prayer that God will direct the group in its discussions and decisions, but what does this prayer really mean? And how is it answered? How does God speak to a church group in its deliberations?

In Acts 1:23-26 there is a clue as to how the apostles felt about the way God spoke to them regarding group decisions. Two names were presented to them as nominees to fill a vacancy created by the suicide of Judas. As the names were presented, the group prayed, "Lord, you know everyone's heart. Show us which one of these two you have chosen to take the place in this ministry and apostleship from which Judas turned aside to go to his own place." The very next sentence following this prayer states, "And they cast lots for them, and the lot fell on Matthias; and he was added to the eleven apostles."

It is apparent that they prayed as a group, and then they voted. Today many Christians believe that God speaks to their congregation or committee likewise by means of a majority vote of those present. Whether or not they realistically believe this has little to do with the matter. This is the way they function. Regardless of how long they may pray about a building site, a slate of officers, or the color of the primary department chairs, the time comes for the vote to be taken. Often this vote is crucial in the life of the church and its entire missionary outreach.

Not only is the outcome of the vote important to the life of the church, but also the way in which the decision is made may have far-reaching effects. A small church in a growing community died because three or four people were allowed to make the monthly business meeting a horrible farce. Through the years responsible persons had left the church until eventually only five persons remained in the congregation. It is highly possible that church members reveal their true selves more accurately at the church business meeting than in church school classes, the worship services, or other occasions of more conscious witness to their Christian faith. Because of this problem, some may be discouraged from entering the Christian ministry, and the giving of some churches is kept at a low level. Indeed, it is possible that some short pastorates can be traced to troublesome church business meetings.

For these reasons church members need to learn and practice the basic rules that are accepted guides for responsible group decision-making. If the congregation believes that God speaks through the majority vote, it must sharpen its long-neglected understanding of parliamentary procedures.

Parliamentary procedure is the process by which a group translates its beliefs into action. For many years parliamentarians have understood that parliamentary law is just common sense used in a gracious manner. Marguerite Grumme has pointed out "The Four Basic Principles of Parliamentary Law:

1. Courtesy and justice for all.
2. Consider one thing at a time.
3. The minority must be heard.
4. The majority must prevail."[1]

If church groups will follow these four basic principles, they will make a long stride forward in changing many meetings from parliamentary chaos to Christian harmony!

The church business meeting is a tremendous

change from most other activities of the church. Instead of agreement and harmony, discussion and debate are the order of the day. There is a very great danger that the meeting will become a competitive situation for the church members because they are unaccustomed to this procedure. They are thrust into competition for the floor, competition for speaking rights, competition in voting. They are not prepared to accept disagreement on issues. To them such disagreement is the same as being opposed to the other *person*. They are distressed to find that one member must vote against the motion of a fellow member. The matter becomes subjective and causes bitter feelings between the members, often over trivial matters.

Church leaders can help to relieve this situation by demonstrating and teaching the difference *between a determined will* and a *permissive will*. In contrast to the determined will, which expresses opinions as though they were fact, the permissive will is the simple expression of opinion as opinion. Knowing the difference and employing the permissive will technique will not only help the tenor of the congregational or committee meeting but its benign influence also will spill over into the rest of life. All human relationships, particularly within the family, are helped by this knowledge. If opinions are expressed as opinions and not facts, a better response will follow.

For example, if someone were to say, "It's too hot in here," another might differ because for that person the temperature might be just right. But, if one says, "It seems too hot to me," no argument can be forthcoming. No one can argue about how a thing seems to another person, but one *can* argue when a statement is blunt and unqualified.

Let each one test his or her own conversational practices and note how often he or she is expressing opinions as though they were facts. The presiding officer can be of help not only in learning to speak in this manner personally but in teaching it to others. Discussion groups, classes, and other informal groups are ideal situations for presenting a discussion of the "permissive will."

The leader can also help the group learn to emphasize areas of agreement rather than those of disagreement. In sermons and addresses a leader can drop hints such as "We should always look at proposals from the standpoint of . . ." or "How much of this proposal can I go along with?" or "With what part of this plan do I agree?" Slowly a group can develop an attitude of looking for agreement.

The leader can almost always help a meeting by stating: "Reasonable people always agree—if they have enough facts." This statement is a shocker, but study the meanings of the two phrases "reasonable people" and "if they have enough facts." Regrettably, far too many small groups make decisions based on the opinion of one strong-willed person. This practice can be halted by the use of the suggested "shocker." If a group is deadlocked, one of two conditions is present: Either the members are unreasonable or they do not have enough facts. Committees and other groups should learn to find the facts regarding the area of concern about which a decision is to be made. Business corporations provide experts in almost every field of concern. Church groups as well should get the facts from experts in the particular fields under discussion. The more facts a committee secures, the more obvious becomes the correct decision. In following this technique, the church must first believe that all the people on the committees and boards are *reasonable*; hence they need to learn that disagreement usually indicates a need for more facts.

A wise pastor will never permit a board or committee to make a decision on the basis of "what the pastor wants." This practice might enhance the pastor's ego, but it is a deadly trap, causing many a pastor to fail in his or her administrative relationships. What the pastor proposes may be the best solution for the church, but the decision *must* be made on the basis of whether the proposal is right, not on the basis of who wants it. If a decision is made because of what the pastor wants, and then the proposal proves to be ill-advised, or if the plan fails or creates a bad situation, the board or committee that made the decision will feel free of responsibility for it because it was what the pastor wanted.Then the pastor is trapped and must defend his or her program. That defensiveness soon colors all that the pastor does, including his or her preaching. The people find that the pastor is preaching at them, instead of to them.

When the pastor finds that he or she is wrong about the suggested proposal, he or she should quickly admit the error to the group. Surprisingly, such an admission actually enhances his or her leadership. It helps the committee to know that they have a leader whom they can trust. They recognize that their leader is big enough and intelligent enough to know when he or she is wrong. It is hard to identify with a person who is "never wrong." It is even harder to identify with, or trust, a leader who is dead-wrong but not big enough to admit his or her errors.

The pastor's greatest challenge in business meetings or in group decision-making is moving from the "tell to" role of the pulpit to the "share with" role of the decision-making group. The wise

and helpful pastor will endeavor to make that
move. Some pastors feel that their leadership is
enhanced by the fact that all of the church boards
and committees are dependent upon *them,*
whereas the very opposite is true! The only way
to develop lay leadership in the church is to let
the laypersons function. They will care more
about that in which they share. Church officers
should be chosen because of their ability to fill a
particular office. It is certainly poor psychology
for a nominating committee to approach a poten-
tial nominee with the plea, "Anyone can do it.
Will you accept nomination?" It is an insult to the
nominee who will think, "If 'anybody' can do it,
why select me?" The committee should approach
the best qualified person and challenge that person with the importance of the job. Then, when
the church has the best available officers, the
pastor should get out of the way and let them
function.

Whenever a decision has been made, the entire group should feel that the best possible judgment has been used to reach a consensus, and
therefore all members will be happy in the decision. If the vote was made out of fear that some
member might throw a tantrum, or to keep peace
by voting the way "one individual" wanted them
to, the decision will not be satisfactory.

Parliamentary procedure is important, not

just because it is parliamentarily correct, but because it is useful in helping church groups reach responsible, satisfactory, and meaningful decisions. If a congregation does not agree with this and does not feel that all things should be done decently and in order, it should, in all honesty, stop praying for God's guidance and leadership in the meetings.

Notes

1. Marguerite Grumme, *Basic Principles of Parliamentary Law and Protocol* (Westwood, N.J.: Fleming H. Revell Co., 1963), 7.

2

Overcoming
Difficult Situations

Have you ever gone home from a church business meeting deeply grieved in spirit and heart
because of the un-Christian conduct of either you
or someone else? Have you ever felt that, of all
places, the church business meeting should be a
place where Christians should act like Christians? Have you wondered why you didn't sleep
well the night before and/or the night after your
church business meeting? This chapter will deal
with the reasons why far too many church business meetings are anything but what they ought
to be.

The Role of the Moderator

The moderator, or presiding officer, of a business meeting is in a unique position to see that

business is conducted fairly and efficiently. Many of the difficult and knotty situations in church business meetings could be avoided if the following suggestions for presiding officers were followed.

1. The presiding officer should request a person who is making a report to the congregation always to stand while doing so, preferably at the front of the room facing the group. If the report requires action by the group after it has been read, the person making the report should remain standing and move its adoption. He or she should continue to remain standing to answer any questions regarding the recommendation. This procedure should be followed for all committee reports so that the presiding officer will not be tempted to answer questions regarding the recommendation.

2. The presiding officer must never enter into debate or discussion while occupying the chair. All parliamentary authorities agree on this important fact. *Robert's Rules* states emphatically the irregularity of this procedure.[2] If the presiding officer does enter into the debate, he or she forfeits the right to preside and can be challenged from the floor. The presiding officer can answer a question relative to the parliamentary status of the motion, or what parliamentary effect its passage would have on pending motions, but his

or her right to speak stops there. The rare exception is when the presiding officer is the only person present who has specific information about the issue. Rather than allowing discussion to continue on such items as the wrong set of dates or places, he or she can supply specific *facts*. The presiding officer should avoid being trapped into answering questions that a committee chairperson or member could satisfactorily answer, even if the presiding officer believes he or she could have answered these questions more effectively. A presiding officer must not take sides in a discussion, and therefore must not engage in the debate.

After a speaker has finished, the officer should remain silent or ask whether there is further discussion. If a comment such as "That's fine" or "Thank you" is made after one speaker, it must be made after all. But if the comment is forgotten for even one speaker, there will be trouble. If the presiding officer must speak to a motion (and this should be a rare occurrence), the chair must be yielded until discussion and action on that particular motion have been completed.

More difficult situations seem to arise from the presiding officer's participation, in one way or another, in the debate than from any other reason. The moderator must never feel that he or she has to enter into debate in order to "push" the program. Under democratic procedures, the group as a whole has the responsibility for creating and carrying out its program. If the group is not functioning in this way, what is happening needs to be analyzed. Either the procedures must be corrected wherever they may be undemocratic, or the group should give up the pretense of being a democratic body.

3. A presiding officer must never give the impression of demanding one's own way. If pleasure or displeasure is revealed by even the movement of an eyebrow, a similar attitude may be elicited from others. Too many presiding officers have the erroneous idea that they are supposed to manage the outcome of the meeting. Such is not the case. The presiding officer functions as a non-playing referee. A baseball fan would be indignant if an umpire helped the second baseman to make a putout, or if the home-plate umpire deliberately got in the way of a runner whose mad dash for home plate might otherwise tie the score. The presiding officer at a business meeting is an umpire who must not give aid to one side or the other. He or she can only answer questions on the parliamentary effect of the motion. The moderator must never comment on the relative worth or value of the motion before the group but allow the group to reach its own decision.

4. To prevent angry outbursts or improper

decorum in a business meeting, the presiding officer should stand to state the motion, sit during all discussions, and then stand again to put the vote.[3] Once having done this, he or she will never return to the old method of standing throughout the meeting. The technique in detail is as follows: After the chair, standing, states the motion and opens it for discussion, the first speaker rises to discuss the motion, and the presiding officer sits. When the first speaker concludes, the presiding officer rises to ask whether there is other discussion. As the second speaker rises to speak, the presiding officer again sits. This procedure is repeated until all discussion is over. Standing, the officer puts the motion for a vote and announces the result. Thus, the presiding officer stands only when he or she must take an active role in the meeting.

This technique of standing and sitting does many things for the presiding officer, for the speakers, and for the members. The simple physical act of rising and sitting draws fresh air into the lungs, which is relaxing. Moreover, for the presiding officer, that which is happening relative to the motion becomes an objective matter instead of a subjective one. When a speaker stands to address the group, he or she is then the only person in the room who is standing, and he or she is speaking *to* the group, not *at* the moderator.

Under these circumstances the speaker will use a different tone of voice and express the way he or she feels about the motion in a much easier and more helpful manner. All of these factors help those present to reach a consensus, which is the purpose of the meeting. The result will make a world of difference in the tone of the meeting and the inner feelings of all of those present in the meeting.

In the light of these four suggestions, it is obvious that the person who is chosen to be presiding officer or moderator should be an individual who has a disposition for fairness and the respect of most of the members of the group. He or she must be a person who can be truly moderate by conducting the meeting as impartially and objectively as is humanly possible during all discussion and voting procedures. It is much more important that the person chosen to be moderator have these qualities of character than have a knowledge of parliamentary law. Usually this kind of person is willing to learn the simple rules of correct procedure. An attorney in the congregation or someone who has had experience in parliamentary meetings of labor organizations would normally make a good presiding officer. Others in the congregation may have gained valuable experience while serving in student or local government or in civic organizations.

As a general rule, the pastor should not serve as moderator of a church if there is anyone else in the membership who can serve with wisdom and judgment in this position. The pastor is pastor to everyone in the congregation, to those who voted for a motion and to those who voted against it. If the pastor serves as moderator in a business meeting where there is strong debate on a matter, even though he or she remains perfectly quiet while presiding, he or she is, in the minds of those who vote on the losing side, identified with the prevailing side. Any moderator is so identified. The problems that arise for the pastor are to overcome the adverse feeling on the part of some in the congregation and to overcome any personal subconscious feeling of resentment toward some who expressed contrary attitudes in the meeting. It may take days or weeks for these deep feelings to wear away, even in a congregation where all the members are loyal to the pastor. However, in some smaller church congregations, the pastor may be the best person for the job in spite of the possible disadvantages.

Attention to details is a very important requisite of a good moderator, whoever he or she may be. Should the moderator feel that procedure is unimportant, and that all that needs to be done is to find out how folks feel and get them to vote, there is sure to be trouble. He or she will also perpetuate the serious problem that is current in church business meetings of members not knowing what is being done because only straw votes are taken. The only way to protect the rights of the members is for the moderator to know the reasons behind the basic rules of business meeting procedure.

A wise moderator will realize that a church business meeting functions informally most of the time. He will permit many freedoms, often use general consent, allow informal discussion, and yet always recognize the beginning of indecorum. He or she will be sensitive to the members, knowing that the rules were made so that the group can function and reach a consensus, instead of the members being made for the rules. The procedural rules were never intended to cramp or impinge upon fair and open discussion. Any time informality threatens to let the meeting get out of hand, however, the moderator may need to call the group back to a stricter practice of the rules.

A newly elected moderator should learn the correct way of stating a motion, of putting the motion to a vote, and of stating the result of the vote. The motion may be stated by saying, "It has been moved and seconded that we . . ." This statement of the motion must be made in order to open it for discussion. It is of primary importance that every motion be correctly stated by the chair. It is the further duty of the chair to restate the motion just before the vote is taken. When the chairperson senses that discussion is over, he or she does not repeatedly ask, "Is there further discussion?" and never asks, "Are you ready for the question?" or, "Are you ready to vote?" The correct statement is "Hearing no further discussion, we are voting on the motion, 'That we . . .' All in favor of the motion will say 'Aye.' Those opposed to the motion will say 'No.' The 'Ayes' have it, and the motion carries" (or whatever action the vote indicates). Because a member can change his or her vote before the declaration of the outcome of the vote, the vote is not complete until the chairperson has made this declaration.

When does the moderator or chairperson vote? Many incorrectly believe that the only time the moderator can vote is to break a tie. This is not true. *The moderator can vote whenever his or her vote will make a difference in the outcome of the vote!* To be sure, voting in the case of a tie is one such instance. The moderator can, moreover, vote to create a tie, and thus cause the motion to be lost. This would prevent a motion from carrying by one slim vote.

If a vote were that close, the motion should probably be reconsidered or referred to a committee for further study. Another instance in which the moderator's vote would make a difference would occur when he or she votes on a motion that requires a two-thirds vote. Finally, in the rare case when no one votes, the moderator could cast the deciding vote, either in the affirmative or in the negative. When a motion is put to a vote there is a result.

By exercising the right to vote when his or her vote will make a difference, the moderator can protect the right of the minority, or in the case when his or her vote completes a two-thirds vote, the moderator makes it possible for the majority to prevail. In voting, as in all else, the moderator's role is to see that there is justice and fairness for all.

Commonly Misused Motions

Picture a group of children starting out to play baseball. One player has a bat, another a ball, another a glove—but not one of them knows how many strikes make an out. Not one of them knows how many outs make an inning. Players who manage to hit the balls don't know whether to run to the right or to the left. Notwithstanding, they proceed to play ball! Church business meetings are not quite that bad, but they are frighteningly close to it!

It is basic to good decision-making that correct rules be followed. Valid and otherwise useful motions are sometimes misapplied. Therefore, in handling a knotty situation in the church business meeting, the presiding officer needs to possess a working knowledge of some of the commonly misused motions.

As a background for discussing the misuse of motions, it will be helpful to review the normal procedure used for a main motion. After gaining recognition of the chair, the person who wishes to make a motion should state the motion clearly. The chair then states the motion and asks for a second. When the motion has been seconded, the chair asks for discussion on the motion. Most motions can be discussed and amended. When the group is ready, the motion is put to a vote by the chairperson. Unless otherwise specified, the motion carries by a majority vote. Exceptions to this general procedure in the case of other motions will be discussed in a subsequent section of this book.

The motion that is probably misused most often is *to lay the question on the table*. It is a good, legitimate motion when it is used correctly, but it is seldom if ever so used. It means to lay the motion aside temporarily while a more urgent matter is handled. This motion cannot be qualified in any manner. There is no such motion as "to table until the next meeting" or to table in any other qualified fashion.

If a person should so make this motion incorrectly, it is the moderator's responsibility to correctly state the motion so that it becomes a motion to *postpone* to a specified time. The motion to table is such a high-ranking motion that it is neither debatable nor amendable, and therefore must be voted upon immediately. Thus, its misuse is dangerous in decision-making bodies.

The most serious misuse of tabling a motion is using it to kill a motion. It was never intended for this purpose. In fact, it actually keeps a matter alive for the current and the next session of the body if the next session comes within three months. Consequently, the use of this motion is obviously disastrous to a group that meets only once a year. At such a meeting anything that is tabled is actually killed.

If the motion to table is used as a killing device, its characteristics of being undebatable and requiring only a majority vote put it in direct conflict with a basic principle. All manuals on parliamentary law agree that any procedure that holds down free debate on a main motion requires a two-thirds vote. (A rising vote is required for all two-thirds votes in order to insure an exact count.)

The minority in any group has no protection against the misuse of the motion to table except the action of a fair and knowledgeable presiding officer. According to some manuals, it is the duty of the presiding officer to rule the motion to table out of order if he or she believes that it is being used to kill. In such a case, the presiding officer can ask the mover of the motion, "What is the urgent business that is to come before us necessitating the temporary laying aside of this main motion?" This disarming question always reveals the real reason for the motion. The presiding officer can then rule the motion out of order and state why. If the maker of the motion questions this ruling, the presiding officer can read the rules regarding the misuse of this motion from the parliamentary manual adopted as the authority by the group.

If it is the desire of a member to kill a certain motion that is before the group, the proper procedure is to offer a motion to *postpone indefinitely*. This motion requires a second. Although it requires only a majority vote, the minority is protected because this type of motion is debatable. If the motion to postpone indefinitely is made, any number of other saving motions can be made in order to save the original main motion; of course, any motion intended to save the original motion must be made while the motion to postpone indefinitely is pending.

If the motion to postpone indefinitely carries, the motion to which it refers is removed from the consideration of the group for that session. It can, however, be reintroduced at the next or another session.

Another little-used motion (and it should remain little-used) is the motion that is actually a demand: *I object to the consideration of the question.* This demand has no place in church business meetings if decorum in debate has become the practice within the group. Such a statement must be made before any debate has begun. It requires no second. It is neither debatable nor amendable. It must be voted on immediately, and it requires a two-thirds vote. If it carries, it removes the motion from consideration. This objection to consideration is used only when a group feels that the motion that has been placed before it, but not yet debated, is too inflammatory in nature to be considered.

Another erroneous concept about church business-meeting procedure is the apparent feeling on the part of some that matters cannot be discussed without a motion and a second. However, most church business meetings function informally. While this does not mean that certain rules do not need to be followed, a little latitude can be given at the point of discussion. Most church groups function quite adequately by allowing informal discussion before a formal motion is made. This informality does not apply to committee recommendations. The committee chairperson who makes the report always moves the recommendation. If someone in a meeting insists that a matter cannot be discussed without a motion, then a motion *to consider the matter* may be made. If this motion carries, discussion can continue. This is much simpler than the alternative—making the motion *to resolve the group into a committee of the whole* where free discussion is allowed. If the group does vote to become a committee of the whole, then it becomes necessary to have a motion to close the committee of the whole and to report the findings. The motion to consider the matter is much easier. As business meetings become more highly organized, virtually all business will arise from boards and committees who present their recommendations as motions.

High on any list of the most common errors made in church business meetings would be the motion *to make the vote unanimous*. This is an impossible motion; it could never be in order. Once a vote has been taken and its result announced, it cannot be made into anything other than what it was. The proper way to try to achieve a unanimous vote is to move *to reconsider the vote*. This motion must be made by someone who voted on the prevailing side. The motion to reconsider requires a second; it is also debatable. This motion carries by a majority vote and places the

main motion back before the body in the precise
condition it was when voted on originally. The
motion to reconsider must be made on the same
day that the original vote was taken.

If a member, realizing that the vote was almost unanimous, wishes the vote to be unanimous, the procedure is for that member to gain
the floor and be recognized by the chair. Upon
rising, the member first states that he or she is
going to move *to reconsider the vote,* giving reasons for doing so. The member says, in effect, that
since the motion did carry, it is the desire of most
of the members that it carry unanimously; it is
often wise to explain at this point why such unanimity would be desirable. The member then
moves to reconsider the vote. Anyone can second
the motion, regardless of which side he or she
voted on. If the motion to reconsider carries and
if the main motion was debatable, discussion can
continue on the main motion. There is always a
chance that the second vote on the main motion
may be further from a unanimous vote than the
first one. The desire for a unanimous vote never
justifies running the risk of changing a strong,
affirmative original vote.

In church business meetings, the subject of a
unanimous vote occurs most often in regard to
the calling of a pastor. Some pastors feel that they
cannot accept the call of a church unless it is a

unanimous call. Such a position is neither theologically nor parliamentarily correct, and it places an unfair limitation on a hard-working pulpit committee. Why should unanimity become the criterion of the Lord's will? Why should any minister feel that he or she must be wanted unanimously by a congregation that is evaluating candidates for the pastorate? Even our Lord did not receive this kind of confidence.

A negative vote at a special meeting to call a pastor is not always a vote against a particular individual. A person in the meeting may cast a negative vote to show opposition to one particular detail of the proposal. Perhaps the person objects to the method of presenting the name of the candidate or to some of the other implications in the call vote, such as moving costs or renovating the parsonage.

It is quite another matter if the call vote is just a bare majority. Few churches or pastors desire to pursue the matter any further when the vote is a bare majority. In this circumstance, the matter is usually settled immediately by making a motion to reconsider, which normally produces a negative vote. If a minister receives at least two-thirds of the votes cast in the call-of-pastor vote, that candidate should not hesitate to accept the call if so desired. For that particular church,

the achievement of even a two-thirds vote might
be a tremendous victory for the pulpit committee.

By following the correct procedures, a church
group can accomplish its business while protect-
ing the rights of each member. Each person in
the business meeting who is a member of the
group has a right to participate in the discussion
and to vote as he or she thinks best.

Other Common Errors

Some of the most noticeable and consistent
errors made in church business meetings and
other church-related decision-making groups are
described in the following paragraphs. They are
not discussed in the order of their frequency or
importance. Groups should note what they consistently do incorrectly and examine some ways
to correct their errors. Of course, they should
correct them in such a way that the group is not
made to feel that the members and their former
leaders have been completely ignorant of the way
to conduct meetings. Rather than telling a group,
"You are doing this all wrong," the wise leader
will help the group to become self-correcting without criticizing the mistakes.

One of these errors is committed when someone speaks without first gaining recognition from
the chair. Unauthorized speaking occurs most
often during debate on a motion. Fundamental to

all good parliamentary procedure is the principle that only one person speaks at a time. Someone must decide who that person is to be; this is a primary function of the presiding officer. He or she must assign the floor. In all church business meetings of more than a dozen persons, anyone desiring the floor must rise and address the chair, saying, "Mr. Chairman," or, "Madam Chairwoman," so the chair can see and hear that person.

There may come a time when three or four persons desire the floor at the same time. Because this can happen, the chair should know how to assign the floor. Just because a person rises does not mean that the chair must recognize that person as the next speaker. The floor is assigned to the first person to stand and address the chair, unless that person has spoken once on the motion and someone else desires to speak, or unless another person has risen at the same time and the presiding officer has reason to believe that this other person will speak on the side of the question opposite that of the last speaker. Insofar as the presiding officer can ascertain, the floor should be assigned alternately to speakers on opposite sides of the pending issue.

A second common error is the outcry from the floor, "Question, question!" Although this is practiced widely and consistently, it is erroneous and

highly discourteous. Never have such outcries
had any place whatsoever in parliamentary procedure. One person crying "Question!" cannot
force the entire group to stop all discussion suddenly and vote. If the chair attempts to ignore
the cry and continues to ask for further discussion, someone almost always says, "The question
has been called for," thus forcing the uninformed
moderator to put the matter to a vote. This action
is wrong. *Robert's Rules* states, "A legitimate
question cannot be suppressed in a deliberative
assembly without free debate, except by a two-
thirds vote."[4] *Demeter's Manual of Parliamentary
Law and Procedure* says, "Outcries of 'I call for
the question!' (or, 'Question!' . . .) are meaningless,
unparliamentary (discourteous, improper) and
unenforceable, and the chair should so inform the
members."[5]

No doubt this discourteous practice grew out
of the improper use of the valid motion, *I move
the previous question.* This motion stops debate
if it carries. It can be made during discussion of
most other motions. It is, however, undebatable
and unamendable. It requires a two-thirds vote
to carry. If it carries, the debate is halted, and
the pending motion is put to a vote. If it is the
wish of a member to halt debate, this is the correct motion to make. However, for church groups,
a better motion to make is one *to limit debate.*

To forestall the outcry of "Question," the chairperson should not use the antiquated form, "Are you ready for the question?" Instead, he or she should always say, "Hearing no further discussion," and then put the motion to a vote. This does not stop anyone who wishes to speak; when the chairperson begins to say, "Hearing no further discussion . . ." any member may rise and address the chair, thus resuming the debate. The wise presiding officer can usually sense when discussion is over and the group is ready to vote.

When the presiding officer hears the outcry of "Question," he or she should state in a kind and tactful manner, "The chair has heard the member call out 'Question.' This only indicates that the member is ready to vote. There may be others who wish to discuss the motion further. Is there other discussion?" This technique will slowly train a group not to use this unparliamentary outcry. It may also encourage some members to review their manuals on parliamentary procedure when they get home. It should be obvious that one person, by saying "Question," cannot halt the discussion and force the vote to be taken. Slowly, and with tact, the group should be reeducated to this understanding. There are good motions to limit debate as well as the motion, "I move the previous question."

Another consistent problem is caused by a

member who discusses something other than the pending motion. Discussion must be germane to the pending motion, but considerable latitude is allowed. However, it is not unusual for discussion to roam too far afield. The most effective help a presiding officer can give in the correction of this error is to state the motion from time to time during the discussion. Occasionally, the situation may dictate the need to do this after each speaker. If the motion is long and complicated, it is the duty of the secretary to write it out and give it to the presiding officer. The chair can also ask the maker of the motion to write out the motion and give it to the secretary.

Parliamentary authorities agree that one of the causes of confusion is the failure of the chair to keep the group fully informed of each step in the parliamentary process as it occurs. The habit of the chair's merely saying, "The motion is carried," and then moving on to something else is not good parliamentary procedure. The chairperson should state what is carried or what is lost or explain the effect a motion will have on pending matters if the motion is subsidiary or enabling in nature.

Neither is it good parliamentary procedure for a member to engage in the intolerable habit of saying, "I so move," after hearing someone discussing something or wondering out loud about the wisdom of something. The maker of a motion should state the motion so that all can hear it and know what the motion is. It is the duty of the chairperson to insist that motions be worded in a positive manner and presented according to the correct procedure; all members must understand clearly what either an affirmative or a negative vote would mean.

A common problem is the monopoly of the discussion by one member. Speakers are entitled to speak twice on the same question on the same day (except on an appeal), but they cannot speak the second time on the same question if a member who has not spoken on that question wishes to speak. Virtually all parliamentary manuals plainly say that if the organization's bylaws do not state otherwise, the length of time a speaker can speak on a motion, at one standing, is ten minutes. This period can be lengthened or shortened for that one meeting, or discussion, by a two-thirds vote of the group assembled.

Another incorrect procedure tolerated in business meetings is allowing the maker of a motion to say, "I _withdraw my motion_ if it is all right with the seconder." Granted, there are times when the maker of a motion, after hearing discussion on it, wishes the motion had never been made. However, the rules about the withdrawal of motions allow the maker of a motion to with-

draw the motion by merely requesting its withdrawal only before it has been stated by the chairperson. After that, it no longer belongs to the
mover, but has become the property of the group.
The seconder has nothing to do with whether or
not the mover can withdraw the motion. One
person does not have the right to take a motion
away from a group that is considering it.

However, after the motion has been stated by
the chair, the maker of the motion can, with the
permission of the group, withdraw the motion.
The mover must ask the chair for permission to
do so. The chairperson, therefore, says to the
group,"The maker of the motion wishes to withdraw the motion. If there are no objections, he or
she will be permitted to withdraw the motion.
Are there any objections?" (Pause) "Hearing none,
the chair declares that it is withdrawn."

This procedure is a perfect example of the wise
use of *general consent* or *unanimous consent*. The
steps in the use of general consent are:

1. State what is to be done if there are no
objections.

2. Ask whether there are any objections.

3. State, "Hearing no objections, the chair declares that it will be so ordered or done." If there
is even one voiced objection, it blocks general
consent. The correct procedure would then be to
have a formal motion to accomplish what is de-

sired, for example, permission to withdraw a motion. When using the technique of general consent, the chair should never appear hurried.

The same procedure of general consent, or a formal motion of permission, can be used to modify a motion. Often, during or after discussion, the maker of the original motion desires to modify the motion to include some of the suggestions brought out in the discussion. The use of general consent would greatly expedite the business before the group, avoiding time-consuming amendment procedures. General consent should be employed only when there seems to be a general unanimity in the group regarding the ideas brought out during discussion. For example, the subject of the main motion may have been the purchase of a used piano. During the discussion a member may express strong feelings that it should be an upright piano and should cost no more than $400. The maker of the original motion can request permission to change the motion to embody these two suggestions. The seconder of the original motion has nothing to do with this request for the privilege to modify one's own motion. The seconder can, however, withdraw his or her second. In this event, another member could second the motion. The presiding officer uses the general consent procedure as outlined above to grant permission to modify the motion.

The goal of group business meetings is to reach a consensus. Everything in parliamentary procedure is aimed at making this possible. Thus, decorum in debate with only one person speaking at a time is important. The general consent procedure, which makes it possible to quickly record formal approval on matters of common agreements, is another aid to reaching a consensus while holding to the axiom that the minority must be heard and the majority must prevail.

Notes

2. Henry M. Robert, *Robert's Rules of Order, Revised* (New York: Scott, Foresman and Company, 1951), 240-241.

3. Robert, *Rules of Order*, 237-238.

4. Robert, *Rules of Order*, 47.

5. George Demeter, *Demeter's Manual of Parliamentary Law and Procedure* (Boston: Bostonia Press, 1961), 231.

3

The Quorum, Order of Business, Reports, Resignations

Church groups need to understand the basic rules regarding a quorum. A quorum is the number of members who must be present in order to conduct a legal business meeting of an organization. This number is usually established in the bylaws of the organization and can be changed by the stated procedure for amending the bylaws. The requirement of a quorum protects the church, or other organization, from a minority action that would be binding upon the whole group.

It is the duty of the chairperson to note that a quorum is present at the beginning of the meeting. Something like the following should appear in the clerk's minutes: "June 22, *a quorum being present*, the regular business meeting opened...." This will establish the legality of any proceeding that may follow, in case documentation should ever be needed in a court of law. If during the meeting the number dwindles to less than a quorum, but no one formally questions the absence of a quorum, common law holds that a quorum was presumed to be present throughout the meeting and all transactions are legal. The minutes establish that a quorum was present at the opening of the meeting and that no one questioned the presence of a quorum before the close of the meeting.

If a quorum is not present when the meeting is opened, the best thing to do is to adjourn. Not only will this eliminate the danger of taking action that might later be questioned, but it will dramatize for the group the problems implicit in the lack of a quorum. It will remind all of the members of their responsibility to be present at business meetings. If this happens repeatedly, such forced adjournment will reveal the need for a revision of the bylaws regarding the number of members needed for a quorum. If the number stated in the bylaws is too high, the only way to show forcefully the need for revising the requirement is to enforce it.

In the absence of a quorum, there are only two things that may be done other than adjourn. The group may recess in order to provide time to secure a quorum. Someone present might volunteer to go around the corner and get Mr. and Mrs. Hardly-Ever-Miss, and their added presence would increase the number to a quorum. Beyond such an action, *Robert's Rules of Order* implies that a group may take emergency action that may be ratified at a later meeting when a quorum is present.[6] Only an extremely urgent matter would dictate that emergency measures be taken in a non-quorum meeting. In no case where the subject matter of the motion is highly controversial would a court of law sustain action taken in a meeting where less than a quorum was present.

In church business meetings, one urgent matter that often faces a non-quorum group is voting on the formal acceptance of new members, with baptism or transfer of letter and the right hand of fellowship scheduled for the next Sunday. In order to avoid this non-quorum problem, a line could be added to the church constitution and bylaws saying, in effect, "Applicants for church membership may be voted upon at any regular business meeting of the church, at any regular Sunday service, or at any regular midweek service of the church."

In this matter of voting upon new members of the church, all should understand that the vote of the congregation in no way reflects any judgment concerning the proposed member's spiritual standing, but deals solely with his or her legal standing as a member of the church, which is a legal organization. In order to be a voting member of an organization, one must be voted into the membership. There will be times when the congregation will be voting on the purchase or sale of real estate, or other legal matters, in which event documentation of the authority of the vote would need to show that such authorization was by vote of the members of the corporation.

In nearly every state, churches are classified as religious corporations (if they have properly followed the procedures of incorporation). If a church is an unincorporated religious society, it cannot hold title to real estate, make contracts, or sue in its own name. The legal title of the property would then be vested in the trustees. Most churches have been properly incorporated, but the time taken to find out is well spent.

Another legal matter that should be carefully checked is the fine print in all of the insurance policies covering church property. In one case a $30,000 pipe organ was specifically excluded from coverage under the fire insurance policy on the church building and its contents. No one was aware of such an exclusion, and all had assumed the organ was insured. When it was discovered, the exclusion was immediately corrected by adding coverage for the organ.

For the sake of order, most groups follow a

regular *order of business* in their meetings. After the reading of the minutes, the first order of business is the presentation of the reports of officers, boards, and standing committees. Normally, these reports are taken up in the order in which the officers, boards, and standing committees are named in the organization's bylaws. Following these reports come the reports of special committees, in the order in which those committees were appointed. Next in line are any special orders, that is, matters of business that were voted to be made special items of consideration and action at this particular meeting. Again, these would follow in the order in which they were referred to this meeting.

After reports and special orders, unfinished business (never called "old business") follows. Unfinished business would be anything pending at the time of adjournment at the last meeting. Other unfinished business would be any matters of business or motions postponed until this particular meeting that had not been made a special order.

If the meeting in question is a *special meeting,* the order of business is determined by the bylaws, which frequently state that no business can be transacted except that business for which the special meeting has been called. Should some other business be presented that is not germane to the special business, it should be halted by someone's rising to a *point of order* and calling attention to the breach of rules. The bylaws cannot be set aside or suspended without following the procedure for amendment that is specified in the bylaws.

In a business meeting, the minutes are usually approved as read or circulated, using general consent for such approval. The treasurer's report is neither approved nor adopted. It is just a report. Therefore, it is proper to thank the treasurer for his or her report, stating that it will be placed on file. The group knows that there will be an annual audit of the treasurer's reports.

Usually it is a rule that unless a committee report contains a motion or recommendation, no action is taken on the report. It is automatically received by the group by hearing it read. A good guide to follow is to remember that, generally, a report containing findings is accepted. Reports that call for action or set forth recommendations are adopted if the members so desire. There may be a rare occasion when the group wishes to indicate its concurrence with a report that calls for no action and reports no findings. In this instance, the group would *vote approval of the committee's work* and thank the committee formally by having it so indicated in the minutes. It is best to remember: Accept findings; adopt recommendations.

A motion that is the result of a committee report never needs a second because the committee recommendation implies that someone other than the chairperson who has made the motion favors the action.

It is not necessary to take the time to get the name of the person who seconds any motion. Seconds to motions only indicate that more than one person favors the proposition. If the motion carries, a second is always implied; and the motion cannot be invalidated later because someone remembers that there was no second.

Resignations are handled in the same way as any other main motion. They can be withdrawn, however, any time prior to their acceptance by the group (which would mean the actual vote). The group can never be a party to any unilateral agreement between two officers who may enter into a private understanding with each other that each will resign if the other will. If one really does resign and the resignation is accepted, the other officer cannot be forced to follow through just because the two officers had a private understanding.

Notes

6. Robert, *Rules of Order*, 173.

4

Handling Amendments

Amendments are excellent tools for correcting motions that are ambiguous in meaning or that may need clarifying or a bit of polishing. A group will usually pass a main motion that it has amended. By the same token, a questionable motion that has not been perfected by the amending process is almost sure to be defeated. A member who opposes a motion that seems destined to pass may try to amend it in such a way as to eliminate the more objectionable part. Actually the objectionable part may be a minor part of the main motion and can be stricken out by amendment.

Group members need to learn to use the amending procedures. Too often, a member will rise to speak against a pending motion and will make some excellent suggestions for improving the motion, but unfortunately that member does not go on to propose an amendment. Whenever a person feels strongly enough about a matter to get up in front of a group to state his or her views, that person should believe in those views enough to make the necessary amendment to project his or her ideas into the main motion.

Rising to make an amendment, the member moves the amendment, remains standing until it has been seconded, then states in a clear, courteous manner why he or she feels that this amendment should carry. Because it is good to begin with a positive statement, the person may explain what is right about the main motion, then what is objectionable, and how the proposed amendment will help to remove the objectionable part. Speaking from the floor will help anyone to grow in leadership ability.

The motion to amend requires a second, is debatable if the main motion is debatable, and is amendable if the amendment is not itself an amendment to an amendment (that is, an amendment of the third degree). A motion to amend requires a majority vote to carry. Naturally, the amendment is voted upon before voting on the main motion. An amendment can be reconsidered until such time as the main motion to which it adheres has been at least partially carried out. For example, the main motion provided that a certain person be appointed to fill the unexpired term of a vacated office, and the amendment was that the person be appointed for three months. Suppose that this action carried and was partially fulfilled in that the appointee was notified of his or her new position. Under these circumstances, the amendment cannot be reconsidered.

The amendment must always be germane—that is, it must add or delete a logical detail—to the main motion. It may be hostile, but it must be germane. The amendment is not germane if its substance could easily be presented later in a separate motion. Much latitude is allowed at this point. The main motion may be "to take the surplus funds in the music committee's treasury and buy a used piano." The amendment might be "to take these funds and buy a stereo for the youth hall." In this case, the amendment would be hostile but germane because the proposal still deals with the use of surplus music funds.[7]

Many people become confused about the need for an amendment to be germane, since legislative bodies often attach unrelated amendments to a main motion. It should be noted, therefore, that such bodies use Thomas Jefferson's *Manual on Parliamentary Law*, and the principles in his manual have been adapted to meet the special needs of these particular groups. The principles stated therein, however, do not apply to church business meetings.

A main motion can be the object of innumerable amendments but cannot have more than two amendments pending at one time: (1) the amendment to the main motion, and (2) the amendment to the amendment. Under parliamentary law, an *amendment of the third degree* cannot be made. This would be an amendment to a pending amendment to an amendment. Thus, a main motion may have an amendment pending. Then a second amendment may be proposed to the first amendment, but a third amendment cannot be accepted until action has been taken upon the second amendment.

A particular form of amendment is the *substitute motion*. This is a motion to amend by striking out the entire wording of the main motion and substituting an entirely new wording. The new wording can even be hostile, but it must be germane.

Handling a substitute motion exactly as an amendment poses some problems because a substitute motion can take precedence over the pending amendments, and this priority often seems unfair to members who have been striving to perfect the motion through the amending process. George Demeter, in his *Manual on Parliamentary Law and Procedure*,[8] meets this problem by suggesting that when a motion to substitute is made and properly seconded, the chair should state the substitute motion. The chair then states that before action is taken on the substitute, the amendments to the main motion are still open to discussion or further amending. When the amending process is finished on the main motion, the chair opens the substitute motion for discussion and amendments, if any. Thus, every member has the right to have his or motion considered fairly by the group. If the substitute motion had been acted upon immediately after it was moved, and it had carried, the original main motion would have been removed from the consideration of the group. When the substitute motion is opened for discussion, the amending process can take place relative to the substitute motion, just as with the original motion.

Finally, when the substitute motion and the main motion have been perfected by means of amendments to the satisfaction of the proponents of each action, the substitute motion is voted upon first. If the substitute motion carries, it is then substituted for the main motion. This means the death of the original main motion and its amendments. Now the newly substituted motion must be voted upon as the main motion because it has been substituted for the original main motion.

Immediately following the passing of a substitute motion and before it is voted on as the main motion, other substitute motions and amendments can be made and acted upon. Each of the newly substituted motions would be voted on before the vote on the new main motion. The vote on the substitute motion as the main motion also gives a member, who may have been opposed to the substitute when it was introduced, a chance to reconsider his or her position in the light of new alternatives. The second vote adopts and legalizes the action indicated in the substitute motion.

Naturally, if the substitute motion failed to carry in the first instance, the chairperson without delay would call for the vote on the main motion as amended and announce the outcome.

Notes

7. Robert, *Rules of Order*, 144-146.
8. Demeter, Parlimentary Law, 75-78.

5

Resolving Complex Issues

There are a number of specialized motions whose function is to facilitate the handling of business by a group. While at first glance they may seem too highly technical to be of value in the average church business meeting, a closer study will reveal their value in piloting a congregation through a complex issue expeditiously with fairness to all.

The first two groups of these motions, the privileged and the subsidiary motions, have a definite order of rank. This means that a motion of higher rank can always be made while a motion of lower rank is pending. By the same rule, a motion of lower rank cannot be entertained while a motion of higher rank is under consideration. Every person in a leadership role should have a parliamentary chart similar to that on the last page of this book, which shows at a glance the rank of motions. The other two groups of specialized motions, the incidental and the restoratory motions, have no inherent rank, but take on the rank of the motion to which they adhere.

Privileged Motions

In order of rank, these are the five privileged motions: (1) to fix a time at which to adjourn, (2) to adjourn, (3) to recess, (4) to raise a question of privilege, and (5) to call for the order of the day. These motions can take privilege only when another motion is pending. If there is no motion on the floor, these motions are to be handled as any other main motion.

The motion *to fix a time at which to adjourn* is very valuable when the time is late and important business is left to be handled. It is important to note that this takes precedence over the motion *to adjourn*. When discussion has been long and heated, there is always the danger that someone will make the motion to adjourn and the rest of the group will assume that because this is a privileged motion, there is nothing further they can do except vote on the motion to adjourn. However, another member can make the motion to fix a time at which to adjourn, thus saving any important business for a later hour or day, and yet complying with the feelings of the exhausted group. Even if the group has already passed the motion to adjourn, this higher ranking motion to fix a time at which to adjourn can still be made if the chairperson has not actually declared the meeting to be adjourned. No vote is complete until the chairperson has declared the outcome. If there is no other motion pending, the motion to adjourn can be amended and debated as any other motion. In practice, it is best to use the general consent procedure for adjournment. Sensing that all of the business that may be brought before the meeting has been concluded, the chairperson can say, "If there are no objections, the chair will declare the meeting adjourned. Are there any objections? Hearing none, the chair declares the meeting adjourned."

The motion *to recess* is self-explanatory. Whenever it seems desirable for the group to take time out, this motion may be made. It requires a second, is not debatable, is amendable as to the length of time to recess, and carries by a majority.

The motion *to raise a question of privilege* pertains to something that may be for the general welfare of the assembly, or it may be personal in nature. A member may address the chair saying, "Mr. or Madam Chairperson, I rise to a question of privilege." When asked by the chairperson to state the question, the speaker replies, for example, "We cannot hear the report. Can the treasurer step to the microphones?" or, "It is too hot in here. Could the windows be opened?" A proper question of privilege may interrupt the speaker and can be made at any time except when higher ranking privileged motions are pending.

The last privileged motion is the *call for the order of the day*. This is helpful only where there is an agenda or order of the day that has been previously adopted by the group. If so, unless the group votes, by general consent or formal action, to change the order of the day, the chairperson must return the meeting to the accepted agenda.

Subsidiary Motions

Subsidiary motions are used to correct, perfect, or to delay action on the main motion. In order of rank, they are: (1) to lay on the table, (2) to call for the previous question, (3) to limit (or extend) debate, (4) to postpone until a definite time, (5) to commit or refer to a committee or board, (6) to amend, and (7) to postpone indefinitely.

The purpose of the motion *to lay on the table* is to lay aside the pending motion temporarily while other, more urgent business is handled. The error of using this motion to kill a main motion without actually bringing the main motion to a vote was discussed in Chapter 2. The motion to table should not be confused with a motion to postpone until a definite time. The motion to table cannot be qualified in any way. Theoretically, it means that the motion will lie on the table, the clerk's desk, or in the clerk's or secretary's care until such time as it may be taken from the table by the vote of the group, if done within three months. After the expiration of that time, the motion, if it is reintroduced, must be considered as a new motion.

The motion *to call for the previous question*, when properly used, can prevent unreasonable delay in meetings by needless repetition of arguments. This motion is a motion to stop debate. The motion to table, or any of the privileged motions, can be made, carried, and ordered after this motion has been made. Thus, there is protection for all groups. If a good motion is about to be talked to death, the motion "I move the previous question" can save the group from endless debate. On the other hand, if the group passes the motion for the previous question, others can move for a recess or adjournment to another time. The motion requires a second, is not debatable, and is not amendable. Because this motion does take away the rights of the group, it requires a two-thirds vote to carry. If it is passed, it can be reconsidered; if it is defeated, it can be renewed or remade following further debate on the main motion.

The third subsidiary motion, *to limit* (or *extend) debate* is useful when greater flexibility is needed in the consideration of a matter. In *Robert's Rules* each speech during debate is limited to ten minutes.[9] Any speaker is allowed to speak a second time on any motion, provided a person who has not spoken does not desire the floor. This motion to limit (or extend) debate can be made to grant each speaker additional time or to allow extra time for debate or to limit the debate to less than ten minutes per speaker or to limit the total time for debate. Because this takes away the rights of the body to free discussion, it also requires a two-thirds vote to carry. It must have a second and is not debatable, but can be amended as to time. If adopted, it can be reconsidered. If it is defeated, it can be reintroduced after there has been additional debate on the main motion or pending amendment.

The fourth ranking subsidiary motion is *to postpone definitely*. This enables the group to postpone further consideration of the pending motion to some later specified time, thus warding off premature action. A definite time must be indicated in the motion, but it must not postpone beyond the next regular meeting. The consideration of the motion that has been postponed until the next regular meeting would come up automatically under unfinished business in exactly the same status it had when postponement was voted. It would still be subject to all of the subsidiary motions or any other perfecting procedures allowable. The motion to postpone definitely must be seconded, is debatable, is amendable, and requires a majority vote to carry. If the motion to postpone includes the qualification to make it a special order of business, then it requires a two-thirds vote. Moreover, this motion may be reconsidered.

The fifth ranking subsidiary motion, *to commit, or to refer*, proposes to have some smaller group or committee consider the matter. If the motion to refer includes instructions to report back to the next business meeting, the committee will be prevented from sitting on the motion without acting upon it. If such instructions are not included, it would be good practice for someone in the group to make an amendment to this effect. The motion to refer requires a second, is debatable, is amendable, may not be postponed, and requires a majority vote. If it is adopted it may be reconsidered, and if it is defeated, it may be renewed after further debate.

The sixth ranking subsidiary motion, *to amend*, has already been discussed in Chapter 4. This motion requires a second, and is debatable. It is amendable itself, unless it is an amendment to an amendment. An amendment cannot be post-

poned by itself. If postponement is voted, it carries the main motion and other adhering motions
along with it. It requires a majority vote; and if
it passes, it can be reconsidered.

The last of the subsidiary motions is the motion *to postpone indefinitely*. This motion can be
used to kill a main motion without bringing the
main motion to a vote. Because it is the lowest
ranking subsidiary motion, any of the other subsidiary motions can be made while this motion is
pending. If any of the other subsidiary motions
is carried, the motion to postpone indefinitely is
removed from consideration. This motion requires a second, is debatable, is not amendable,
cannot be postponed, requires a majority vote,
and may be applied only to main motions. An
affirmative vote can be reconsidered, but a negative vote cannot. Because it is debatable, the motion to postpone indefinitely has the effect of
opening up debate on the main motion for those
who have used up their opportunities for debate
on the main motion itself. A motion that has been
postponed indefinitely can be reintroduced at a
later session.

Incidental Motions

One helpful incidental motion is the motion
to consider paragraph by paragraph or *to divide
the question*. This motion means that the mover

feels that the main motion is too cumbersome and complicated and therefore should be divided so the assembly can vote on each part of the motion separately. The test as to whether or not a motion can properly be divided is: If one part fails to carry, can the other parts stand alone? If so, the question may be divided.

Another often-used incidental motion is the motion *to close the nominations. Reopening the nominations* is also accomplished by an incidental motion.

The motion *to appeal from the decision of the chair* falls within the category of incidental motions. If the chair has ruled on a point of order and a member feels the ruling to be incorrect, that member may move to appeal from the decision of the chair.

When rising to appeal a ruling of the chair, it is wise to refer to the manual on parliamentary procedure recognized in the bylaws, calling attention to the specific rules in question. This makes the unpopular act of rising to a point of order appear reasonable and wise. Hearing a second, the chairperson states: "It has been moved and seconded to appeal from the decision of the chair. The question is: 'Shall the decision of the chair be sustained?' Is there any discussion?" However, this appeal is not debatable if the group has just voted to stop debate on the previous question, or if the immediately pending motion is not debatable. Also, if it relates to a transgression of speaking or indecorum, to allow debate would defeat the purpose of the appeal. When the ruling of the chair has been appealed and it is debatable, the chair can speak two times and other members can speak just one time. In this situation the chairperson can speak in defense of his or her ruling from the chair.

The correct way to put the vote when the ruling of the chair has been appealed is: "Shall the ruling of the chair be sustained? All in favor will say 'Aye.' Those opposed will say 'No.' The 'Ayes' ('Noes') have it, and the ruling of the chair is sustained (reversed)." If the "No" vote carries, the chair must sustain the point of order, changing his or her ruling.

Withdrawing one's motion is an incidental motion. Once the chair has stated a motion, it has become the property of the group and can be withdrawn only with the consent of the group. Again, if this cannot be handled by general consent, it must be a formal motion requesting permission to withdraw the motion in question. No second is required; it is not debatable or amendable; it passes by a majority vote.

During discussion a member often wishes to read from a paper or book. This is not permissible under the generally accepted rules of debate. The member can move to be given permission to so read. This request could be easily handled by general consent or by a simple incidental motion, carrying by a majority vote.

The motion *to choose a certain method of voting* is an incidental motion. If the usual method of voting is by voice vote, a member may wish to move that the method of voting on a particular motion be by a standing vote or by ballot. Such a motion would require a second and is not debatable, but is subject to amendment as to method of voting. A majority vote is required to pass this incidental motion on the method of voting.

If, in a church business meeting, the matter before the group could be clarified by technical information, a member can request that a nonmember who is a professional in the field be allowed to speak, bringing his or her knowledge before the group. This request can be handled by general consent or by a simple motion.

One of the most valuable parliamentary tools is called *filling the blanks*. A church group may have before it a motion to take a certain action. The group is almost unanimously in favor of the action, but there are details upon which there is a wide difference of opinion. For example, suppose the motion is to paint the primary department chairs. However, some like the color blue, others want yellow, and Mr. Eyes-on-the-Budget believes that they should use up the leftover brown paint, which is stored under the Christmas decorations in the attic. Because the association Christian education committee will be guests in the church the following week, there is no time to refer the matter to a committee. Thus, a member may move, "Mr. or Madam Chairperson, I move that we paint the primary chairs, leaving the choice of color blank, then proceed to fill the blank." This motion may be seconded, discussed, and voted upon, putting the group on record in favor of painting the chairs. Then nominations for various colors may be made. The first color to receive a majority vote will be the one that shall fill the blank. Then the group must vote on the completed motion with the blank filled to make the action final. Some parliamentarians do not feel that any vote on the main motion should take place until the blank is filled. Either method is in harmony with the accepted rules of order.

This same technique can be used when the vote to buy or sell something that belongs to the church. If the church is selling something, the voting begins with the lowest price first because more members will probably want to sell for a larger figure. On the other hand, when buying, the voting begins on the largest sum and moves to the smaller amounts.

The incidental motion *to suspend the rules* does not suspend the organization's constitution or bylaws, but only the rules of order for a particular matter currently pending. If, for instance, a high ranking motion such as the previous question had been ordered, no motion below it in rank could be made. For example, it would not be possible to move to refer the matter to a committee. In this case, a member can move to suspend the rules, with the explanation that the intention is to make possible the referral of the matter to a committee. This motion to suspend the rules requires a second, is not debatable or amendable, and requires a two-thirds vote. Suspending the rules can save important matters that are headed for premature defeat without adequate consideration.

Restoratory Motions

Another group of specialized motions are those that have been termed "restoratory" by George Demeter.[10] Their general purpose is to restore matters, to make them as they were prior to the final previous action on the motion. There are four of these motions: *to reconsider*, *to rescind*, *to ratify*, and *to take from the table*. They can be highly beneficial in the correcting of errors in judgment that may have led to premature action on other motions, and in enabling all the members of the group to feel that they have had every opportunity to exercise their democratic rights.

The purpose of the motion *to reconsider* is to bring back before the group for more thought and consideration a motion that has been hastily passed or defeated. This motion must be made by a person who voted on the prevailing side when the motion was previously voted upon. The chair has the responsibility of ascertaining whether or not the mover of the motion actually voted on the prevailing side. Anyone can second the motion regardless of which side he or she favored in voting. The motion is debatable, but not amendable. It requires only a majority vote to carry, and cannot itself be reconsidered.

If the motion to reconsider passes, the motion to which it refers is before the group again for discussion, consideration, amendment, and finally a vote. If the motion to reconsider fails, then nothing more can be done. No motion can be reconsidered twice.

Sometimes, in order to "cinch" a motion, a person who favors the motion and has voted for it will immediately move reconsideration after the chairperson announces that the motion has carried. Naturally, this motion to reconsider is defeated, and the original motion is cinched because reconsideration cannot be moved a second time. However, if the original main motion is opened for reconsideration and is substantially amended, it may be reconsidered again.

The motion to reconsider can be made only at the same meeting or session at which the vote to which it refers was taken. It is valuable if in the same meeting facts or feelings are revealed that show that the original action on the motion was unwise. Then a motion to reconsider will open up the matter for further discussion on the basis of the new information or feelings.

Another facet of this motion may occasionally be used in extreme circumstances. This is the motion *to reconsider and enter*. This means that a member who has voted.on the prevailing side may rise and state, "Mr. or Madam Chairperson, I move *to reconsider and enter*." If this is seconded, it will be entered on the clerk's minutes that at the next meeting the motion is to be reconsidered. No actual vote on reconsideration is taken until the next meeting. If the motion to reconsider is not taken up at the next meeting, it is dead, and the vote on the original motion stands. This provision makes it possible to prevent execution of a matter authorized by the original motion until reconsideration can take place at the next meeting.

The second of the restoratory motions is the motion *to rescind* or *to repeal*. This cancels the action on a vote previously taken at a meeting.

Naturally there would never be a motion to rescind a negative vote on a motion. The easiest and most expeditious way of correcting an erroneous and premature negative vote is to reintroduce the motion at the next meeting. This is done by simply making the same motion over again at the next or any subsequent session.

Anyone, regardless of how he or she voted on the original motion, can make the motion to rescind. It requires a second and is debatable and amendable. It must have a two-thirds vote to carry. The motion to rescind is subject to the motion to reconsider. If notice is given that at the next business meeting a motion will be made to rescind an action just taken, this motion to rescind will require only a majority vote to carry at that meeting. A motion to rescind cannot, however, be made while the original motion is under the notice of a motion to reconsider and enter. If the motion to reconsider fails, then the motion to rescind is in order.

It is not possible to rescind every motion. If, following affirmative action by a deliberative body, that which was adopted is carried out, the group cannot vote to rescind what has already been carried out. For instance, if the motion had authorized the building of a new garage on the parsonage lot and a contract had been signed, the church could not vote to rescind the motion.

A most important restoratory motion is the motion *to ratify*. The purpose of this motion is to legalize a motion or resolution that was voted upon without the authority of the organization. Nothing that is illegal or contrary to the organization's constitution and bylaws can be ratified. The motion to ratify requires a second; it is debatable; it is amendable; and it carries by a majority vote. In church groups, ratification is most often used to confirm or legalize action taken at a meeting where a quorum was not present.

It is also valuable to use the motion to ratify when some church officer has taken action on his or her own initiative in behalf of the church. For example, a trustee may have been aware that the church wanted to buy an electric range for the kitchen. At a sale that person saw a range judged to be ideal. After buying it, the trustee now has to seek ratification of the purchase by the board of trustees. If they fail to back the purchase, the buyer would be individually responsible for the purchase. Or, at a town meeting, the pastor might pledge, on behalf of the congregation, a contribution of $100 toward a community youth center. At the next monthly business meeting, the pastor asks the group to ratify the contribution, but they do not. The pastor has to pay the $100 out of his or her own pocket as a result of taking an unwarranted liberty in making the decision.

The fourth of these restoratory motions is the motion *to take from the table*. This can be used to bring back for discussion a matter that has been tabled in the same meeting or at a meeting within the past three months. If the matter has been tabled for more than three months, it can be brought before the group only by reintroducing the motion itself. The motion to take from the table requires a second and is neither debatable nor amendable. It is carried by a majority vote. If it carries, the motion previously tabled is restored before the group in the same condition as it was when it was tabled. If the motion to take from the table should fail to carry, the original motion can be reintroduced, even in its original wording.

Notes

9. Roberts, *Rules of Order*, 39 and 178.
10. Demeter, *Parliamentary Law*, 137.

6

Nominations and Elections

Church congregations cannot afford to be careless in the nomination and election of their officers. It is vitally important that church officers be legally elected. At some future time the church clerk may need to provide certification of their election, including a copy of the minutes of the meeting in which the account of the election is given. An attorney, for instance, searching the transfer of property by deed would want to guarantee his or her client that the trustees had the legal right to sign the deed transferring the property. If the attorney discovered that these trustees had not been elected legally, he or she could not assure the purchaser of the property that the title or deed was free and clear.

The solution to such a problem might not be difficult, but it could be embarrassing and costly.

It would require going into court and having the so-called election declared a *de facto* election. This would remove the cloud and legalize the right of the trustees to sign the deed. But why not elect the officers correctly in the first place?

In most groups a nominating committee is appointed or elected some time before the election of officers. Usually the bylaws indicate how this committee is to be chosen. The duty of this committee is to prepare a slate of officers for nomination and election. Usually this means one slate of officers. However, it may be necessary according to some church bylaws for the committee to submit two slates of nominees. This is often regarded as a technicality, and two identical slates of officers are submitted. Other nominations can always be made from the floor. Of course, the submission of identical slates would be impossible if the bylaws are so worded as to require the committee to submit two different slates of nominees. This restriction places difficult limitations on the committee. It is far better to allow the committee the freedom of responsibly nominating one slate of officers.

At the time of the report of the nominating committee to the congregation, the chairperson of the committee makes the report to the assembled group. No motion of any kind should be made following this report. The reading of the committee's report automatically places in nomination the names that the committee suggests.

If the actual election is to take place immediately following the nominating committee's report, the presiding officer steps forward and states: "These names are in nomination for these respective offices. Are there other nominations from the floor?" It is not necessary to call for nominations from the floor for each and every office. Be certain, however, that time is allowed for nominations from the floor. The wise presiding officer will refuse to be rushed at this point. He or she will tactfully refuse premature motions to close the nominations by indicating that the motion was heard and will be entertained in just a moment, and asking again, "Are there further nominations?" The presiding officer then states the motion that the nominations be closed. This motion requires a two-thirds vote, as does any motion that takes away the rights of the group. An easier way to close the nominations is for the presiding officer to use the general consent procedure after adequate time has been given for nominations from the floor. To do this, the presiding officer states: "If there are no objections, the chair will declare the nominations closed. Are there objections? Hearing none, I declare that the nominations are closed." The nominations can still be reopened by a two-thirds vote if the group later desires to do so.

Slipshod election procedures in church groups may only succeed in placing nominees on the ballot without ever officially completing the elections. Upon the closing of the nominations, therefore, in a group where the election is to follow immediately, the group must proceed to vote on these nominated officers. When there is only one nominee for each office, a single motion that all nominees be elected is sufficient. Or, upon closing the nominations, the chairperson can state, "All in favor of electing these nominees will say 'Aye.' Those opposed will say 'No.'" If the Ayes have it, the chairperson must declare the officers elected because the election is not complete until the presiding officer has declared that the officers have been elected.

If the bylaws call for a vote by ballot, the ballots should be ready for distribution so that the members may vote without delay. When the ballots have been counted, the results are announced and the officers declared elected.

Never is the motion in order that states, "I move the nominations cease and the clerk be instructed to cast a unanimous ballot." In spite of common practice, such a motion is never in order because it means that by a mere majority vote a group attempts to show unanimous support of the ballot. If the bylaws do not prohibit it, and there is only one nominee for each office, the motion "I move that the nominations cease and the clerk cast the ballot" is in order. This motion requires a standing, two-thirds vote. If the result is not immediately apparent, there is a quick way to determine the outcome. Double the number of negative votes received. If this figure equals or is less than the total affirmative vote, the motion has carried by at least a two-thirds vote. If the negative vote, doubled, is more than the affirmative vote, the motion has been rejected.

If this vote to close the nominations and to instruct the clerk to cast a ballot for the nominees does receive at least a two-thirds vote, the chairperson will state, "The affirmative has carried. The clerk will please cast the ballot." The clerk will stand and state, "I hereby cast the ballot." The chairperson will then declare the officers elected. These statements by the clerk and the chairperson are mandatory.

If the bylaws state that election shall be by a majority of the ballots cast, the procedure outlined above may be followed because the ballot cast by the clerk is a majority of one. However, there are two cases where this procedure cannot be used. The first is the situation in which the bylaws state that election shall be by ballot and by a majority vote of the members present. In this case, the clerk cannot cast the electing ballot even though he or she is unanimously instructed to do so.

Churches should take the necessary action to see that their bylaws on election procedures have wording to this effect: "In the event there is but a single nominee for each office, the clerk may be instructed by vote of the members present to cast the electing ballot." Or they may read: "A secret ballot shall not be required when there is but one nominee for each office. The election may be by voice vote; and if such is in the affirmative, the chair shall declare the nominees duly elected."

The second is the situation involving nominations from the floor. In this case, all nominees for all offices must be listed on the ballot. These ballots are given to the tellers who have been appointed by the chairperson to aid in the voting procedure. When they distribute ballots to the members, each teller should be accountable for a definite number of ballots. A teller should distribute one and only one ballot to each of the valid members assigned to him or her. There must be no other business taking place while the members are voting. The chairperson can cast a secret ballot along with those of the other members. When voting is completed, the tellers gather the ballots, which are then tallied. The chief teller reports the results of the counting of the ballots to the presiding officer, who, in turn, reports the results to the group and declares the officers elected. It is not necessary for the presiding officer to indicate the number of votes cast for each nominee unless requested to do so.

If by some quirk of circumstance there is a tie for one office when voting by ballot, the chair calls for another ballot on just that one office. The presiding officer cannot vote to break this tie if he or she has already voted by secret ballot along with the rest of the group. This second vote is consistent with the general axiom that parliamentary law is common sense used in a gracious manner. The ballots are distributed and the vote taken as before. This procedure usually decides the tie; but if a tie still results, then the decision may be made by *lot*, that is, flipping a coin or drawing straws. According to some parliamentarians, this procedure can be established in the bylaws or by other action of the group prior to the taking of the vote.[11]

If the bylaws call for a period of time to elapse between the report of the nominating committee and the election, no motion is made following the reading of this committee's report. The presiding officer merely thanks the chairperson and states the time and the date when the election will be held. In large groups, the members will receive a printed copy of the nominating committee's report. When the actual time of election comes, much the same procedure as already described is followed except that the nominating committee chairperson reads the list of nominees again before the presiding officer calls for nominations from the floor.

Usually new officers take over in church groups at the beginning of the new church year for which they are elected. The bylaws ordinarily spell out this matter. Some bylaws state that the officer shall be elected for a specific period of years or "until a successor is elected." In the latter event, the newly elected officer takes over immediately following the election to succeed or fill an unexpired term. Otherwise, the new officer takes office at the beginning of the new term. In formal meetings and especially larger meetings, all newly elected officers are installed and take office following their installation.

Notes

11. Demeter, *Parliamentary Law*, 187. See also O. Garfield Jones, *Parliamentary Procedures at a Glance* (New York: The Meredith Publishing Co., 1949), 21.

7

Boards and Committees

Much of the preliminary discussion of church, congregational, and group business is carried out in boards and committees. This vast area of procedure, therefore, should be carefully considered. These smaller groups are also excellent places where good principles of procedure and leadership may be taught in an informal fashion.

Proper Procedures

Regular boards and committees are usually provided for in the church's constitution and bylaws. The areas of responsibility and the number of members on such boards and committees are also set forth. Boards and committees are established by an organization to help it carry out its purpose. Many functions are, and should be, left to responsible committees to perform.

A church business meeting should not have to waste its time deciding what to do with the birthday money or any number of other small, routine matters that can be time-consuming. Any responsible board or committee will always be conscious of the overall direction in which the congregation is and has been moving and will function within that framework. If and when a board or committee decides to move in a direction that it knows to be contrary to the established policy of the congregation, it should bring the matter as a recommendation to the regular church business meeting.

Most churches have the following regular or standing boards: deacons or elders, trustees or vestry men, and Christian education. They also have standing committees for music, missions, finance, social fellowship, and visitation work. Many churches have still more. Some congregations find a great advantage in having a "One-Board System." This one board is made up of members of varying talents who hold responsibility as deacons or trustees, or in finance, music, or visitation. Under this system, the members do not have to run around to seek approval from several other boards or committees before taking action.

No board or committee has authority beyond that which is conferred upon it by the bylaws of the group that brought it into existence. The duties of a board should be clearly spelled out in the bylaws. Every board member has the right to know what the duties and limitations of his or her board are. Much of the difficulty that arises in local church business meetings could be avoided if every member had a clearer understanding of the duties of boards and committees.

There is much value in the monthly or quarterly meeting of an advisory board made up of all the standing boards and committees of the church. In such a meeting, which comes at a time shortly before the monthly or quarterly congregational meeting, the recommendations of the various boards would be heard and discussed. This procedure would give a wider understanding of the matters that are to come up for final approval at the congregational meeting. It is preferable to discover the flaws in a proposition in such a meeting rather than to expose them in the general congregational meeting. This procedure gives each board enough time to improve its recommendations as much as possible before the final presentation for formal action.

Certain rules that apply to boards and committees should be learned and observed. To begin with, the chairperson has the right, along with the other board or committee members, to make motions, discuss motions, and vote, without leaving the chair. This is possible only in a board or committee that is small. In *Robert's Rules of Order, Revised*, a small board or committee is defined to be one of approximately a dozen persons.[12] In larger boards or committees the same rules are used as those that apply in a regular business meeting. In small committee and board meetings the members do not need to rise to speak; a second to a motion is never needed; and anyone can propose reconsideration of a passed motion. In other words, a committee or small board functions in a much more informal fashion than a regular business meeting.

Any organization may, through its bylaws, specify certain rules or procedural methods for its committees or boards. However, in the absence of such rules, the committee or board can function with all of the freedom indicated in the preceding paragraph. There is no limit on the number of times a member may speak in a board or committee meeting, provided everyone who wishes to speak has the opportunity to do so. In small groups there is no limit on the length of time a member may speak. A board or committee cannot impose such limits on itself except by unanimous consent or vote.

Usually all boards and standing committees are elected in accordance with the bylaws of the organization. Special committees are normally appointed by the presiding officer of the organization. It is common, but incomplete, for a member to move that a motion be referred to a special committee for study. This motion leaves out vital factors, thereby provoking needless discussion, amendments, and other time-consuming tactics. The *motion to refer* should be worded in this fashion, "Mr. or Madam Chairperson, I move that this motion be referred to a special committee of three persons to be appointed at this meeting by the chair, and that this committee be instructed to report back at our next regular meeting." Such a motion includes the number of members proposed for the committee, how the committee is to be selected, when the special committee is to be appointed (extremely important), and when the committee is to report back to the group. Without these four elements the motion is ambiguous, and the group is forced to waste time discussing and amending each part.

Most referred motions can be handled by a standing committee. When a special committee has been appointed, either by the chair or by nomination and vote, it is the duty of the secretary (clerk) to notify those appointed. The person named first is the convener of the committee's first meeting. The committee may elect its own chairperson. It is not always wise for the presiding officer to appoint the chairperson of a special committee. If the presiding officer is instructed by the group to appoint a committee chairperson, then of course he or she should do so. Otherwise, each special committee should be permitted to select its own chairs.

If the chairperson of a small committee senses that there is general unanimity in the group after the discussion on an item of business is completed, he or she should use general consent to arrive at the decision of the group. Once this technique is used, the decision is reported as being unanimous. It is not always necessary to keep formal minutes in a committee, but someone should be asked by the chairperson to record correctly the actions taken by the group. When the reports or recommendations are made to the larger body, the actions agreed on by the members of the committee can then be reported accurately.

Sometimes the members of a committee will not agree on the report they wish to make to the parent body. If the minority feel very strongly about their position, they have the freedom to present their point of view before the larger body. The most expeditious way to proceed is for one person chosen by the minority group of the committee to be ready to gain the floor immediately after the chair has stated the recommendation of the committee. Gaining the floor, the member makes a substitute motion that the minority report of the committee be adopted. This person then speaks in favor of the report. It is subject to all of the debate and amending procedures of any other motion. Then the minority report is voted on before the majority recommendation, because it has the rank of an amendment or substitute motion.

Actually, a minority report rarely carries. It does, however, serve the important purposes of holding the idea before the group that the minority must be heard and of giving the majority group an idea of the relative strength favoring their recommendation. It may guide the majority to modify their recommendation by adding a helpful or clarifying amendment. Such action could mold the two opposing sides back into a single unit. This is highly appropriate in a church business meeting where, more than in any other kind of business meeting, there must, if possible, be a resulting consensus.

Sometimes the pastor, or board chairperson, or some other officer will be designated as an ex officio member of a committee. The term *ex officio* means "by virtue of the office." Consequently, an ex officio member of a committee has the same rights as any other member of the committee. He or she can make motions, enter into the discussion, and vote. The only difference in this person's status from the other members on the committee

is that he or she is not counted in determining
the presence of a quorum of the committee or
board.

Usually it is understood that a quorum of a
committee or board is a majority of its members.
If a committee consistently lacks a quorum, the
group may be meeting on the wrong night, or the
wrong people may have been placed on the committee. The only way to correct this situation is
to enforce the quorum rule and so bring to light
the real reason for the failure to have a quorum.

Leadership Development

A strong leader is devoted to the development
of leadership ability within the whole committee
or board. One of the best methods of achieving
this is to permit the board to function. The board
members may make mistakes, but, as in every
group large or small, if a group is permitted to
function according to its bylaws, it will be self-
correcting. The leader must believe this or face
his or her own hidden disbelief in the democratic
way of decision-making.

In most churches the bylaws provide that the
pastor shall be an ex officio member of all boards
and all committees. As an ex officio member, the
pastor has the same right to make motions and
to discuss matters as any other member. When
some matters come before the board, the wise

pastor will refrain from entering the discussions, recognizing that a pastor's opinion may carry more weight than that of the other members of the board or committee. There are always committee members who will fall in line with the pastor's position regardless of what it is. Pastors must recognize this fact and judiciously exercise their right to discussion on boards and committees so that they cannot be accused of dominating the group.

By speaking on every matter up for consideration, a pastor may, without meaning to do so, create the impression of being an expert whose recommendations must be implemented. No pastor should be caught in the deadly trap of allowing a committee or board to make its decision on the basis of "this is what the pastor wanted." A wise pastor will, however, express his or her opinions on some matters in board meetings. The board has the right to expect the pastor to provide such leadership. The pastor's expressed opinions should *in no way* place pressure on the board so that when the pastor speaks, all are made to feel that the pastoral opinion is an announcement directly from heaven and that for anyone to feel otherwise on the subject indicates rebellion against God, who has spoken through God's servant.

These precautions also apply to the chairperson of the committee, who has more power and authority than the other committee members. Therefore, he or she must use this power wisely without being caught in the trap of attempting, perhaps unconsciously, to shape the decisions of the other board or committee members. He or she may feel that this is evidence of strong leadership, but it is exactly the opposite. No one is smart enough to know all there is to know on every subject, so the chairperson and the pastor must rely on the judgment of other members of the committee or board. These other members may have far more experience and knowledge of the matter under discussion than either the chairperson or the pastor.

One means of helping the group to get their work done is the method of establishing priorities at the beginning of each church year. Because of the informal nature of most church board or committee meetings, much time is wasted on unimportant matters without ever getting around to vital matters. For instance, a board of trustees can spend all its time dealing with small matters and then suddenly realize that it is ten o'clock, and they have not begun to discuss the leaking roof.

The technique for arriving at priorities at the beginning of the church year works like this: In each board, after the opening prayer and call to order, each member, supplied with a paper and pencil, is encouraged to go off to a private place. There he or she should think of the things that need to be done and write down, in order of importance, the six things he or she feels the board should accomplish during the next year. The board members will heartily rise to this challenge and will take this experience seriously.

When the lists are completed, they are returned unsigned, placed in the center of the table, and there read aloud by one person. Another person, usually the secretary, records the items, noting the number of times each one is mentioned. This enables the board members to see objectively what each of them really considers to be priorities. The items of greatest concern are those that appear near the top on the largest number of individual lists. The six items mentioned most often become the first six items to be considered by that board. By secret ballot the board votes on these six items, giving each one a rank. When the tabulation of these ballots is completed, the board formally designates the top three priority items for immediate action. The remaining three items of high priority will be handled by the board later during the course of the year.

This technique of establishing priorities has several advantages. It saves time in each meeting; apart from emergency situations that may arise, decisions concerning the agenda have already been made. The list of priorities gives the group a standard by which they can measure their progress during the year. At the same time, an overbearing person (whether the pastor, the chairperson, or someone else) cannot dominate the work of the board since each member participated in the decision that determined what the main goals and projects of the board would be. Whenever the group begins to stray from the subject, the leader can remind them of their own list of priorities.

There is another important principle of group procedure: When a decision is made, enabling action should accompany it. This involves a vote as to who is to do it, how much money is to be spent, or when it is to be done. If the proposed action requires congregational adoption, these enabling features should be included in the report. By so doing, the proposed action will be greatly expedited and clarified.

When a board votes to do something, the chairperson should appoint some person to get the task under way—for example, secure bids, select colors, or employ workers. This gets the work done. Even when it is a routine matter, someone other than the pastor should be appointed to do it. While it might be easier for the pastor to do it, it is a matter of good training to appoint another person to follow through on board action. It saves the pastor from appearing to run everything and allows the board to carry out its own decisions and to function on its own.

The energetic pastor who attempts to do everything single-handedly not only produces a church with weak muscles but also creates a harmful situation. At first, when the pastor does the board's work, his or her eagerness is usually appreciated. However, it is not long before the board begins to feel a bit of resentment toward the pastor's usurpation of their functions. As long as "the pastor does all the decision-making and the work," the board members feel completely useless. This kills board creativity and eventually boxes the pastor into a corner from which the only escape is a move to another church where, too often, the vicious circle begins again.

Pastors will be more highly appreciated if they put ten people to work than if they do the work of ten people. Probably the greatest challenge to leadership is guiding a group to become self-sufficient. One way pastors can help boards and groups achieve self-sufficiency is by encouraging them to include enabling action in their motions whenever necessary. A pastor's leadership is not determined by how dependent the boards and committees are upon that pastor, but by how well the board members can function on their own.

The pastor or chairperson committed to good group decision-making procedure will find the best teaching opportunities in small committee meetings. In the small group it is easy to explain why certain rules of procedure are necessary. The importance of each committee member's being ready to answer questions regarding the recommendations of his or her own committee can be explained. In small group meetings these important things can be taught as incidentals, and they will later filter through the entire church. The key to improving church business meetings lies with the church's boards and committees. It is in these small groups that good procedure begins.

Notes

12. Robert, *Rules of Order*, 208.

8

Conventions, State and National Assemblies

The same rules of parliamentary procedure that are used in church business meetings also apply to the business meetings of state and national denominational conventions and other large assemblies. In addition, there are some special problem areas that are much more likely to be evident in these larger meetings. Because resolutions often take up so much time in a convention meeting, the proper way of handling them will be discussed in the second section of this chapter.

Specific Features of Large Assemblies

In a convention, delegates are apt to be confused by the distinction between *meeting* and *session*. A session may consist of several business meetings that may be scheduled over several days. Each of these meetings, separate in time, is recessed until the next meeting. The adjournment does not occur until the conclusion of the last meeting of the session. However, someone may make a motion to adjourn one of the meetings within the session until some specific date and time. This is an application of the privileged motion to fix a time at which to adjourn. In this case, when the convention meets again at the specified time, it is still in the same session. In a session of several meetings, if a group has voted in one of the first meetings of the session to table a motion, it may vote to take the same motion from the table in a subsequent meeting within the session. But if the next meeting does not come within three months of the meeting at which the motion was tabled, the motion dies. Thus, another session, meeting a year later, could not vote to take such a tabled motion from the table. However, at that time a new motion embodying the old motion could be introduced for consideration.

Working with an adopted agenda or program is another feature that usually distinguishes the convention from the church business meeting. When a convention adopts a program, that program becomes the order of the day, which can be changed only by general consent or a formal motion to change the agenda. The easiest way to change the agenda is through the use of general consent. For example, if a certain speaker must catch a certain plane, then the chairperson can introduce the general consent procedure so that Dr. Hasta Catcha may speak at seven o'clock instead of eight o'clock. As in all cases where general consent is used, if there is an objection, a formal motion and a second is necessary. This motion to change the agenda requires a two-thirds vote. The only exception to this procedure of changing the agenda would be if the motion by which the agenda had been adopted at the beginning of the meeting also included a provision allowing the chairperson or program committee to change the agenda if necessary. To change the agenda arbitrarily is to deprive the members of their rights.

The presiding officer has the responsibility to see that the assembly keeps to the order of business. If he or she fails to do this and the discussion goes beyond the allotted time, a member can *call for the order of the day*. This demand must be recognized unless a privileged motion is before the assembly. Whether the chairperson or a member notes the need to recognize the order of the day, one of two things must be done. Either the chairperson must go on to the next item of business on the program or seek a change in the agenda. He or she may say, "If there are no objections, we will extend the business meeting for thirty minutes. Are there any objections? Hearing none, the chair extends the time for thirty minutes." If there were objections to this general consent, then the chairperson would have to seek a formal motion. If the motion fails to receive the necessary two-thirds vote, the chairperson must then return to the agenda as adopted by the group. Thus the ultimate responsibility for the agenda rests with the assembly.

In a large convention meeting, it is particularly important that the group not waste time in getting the name of the seconder of a motion unless this is specifically required in the bylaws. The only purpose of requiring a second to any motion is to inform the group that the motion is supported by at least one other person. This attempt to get the name of the seconder shows immaturity in correct parliamentary procedure. Parliamentary law does not require that the name of the seconder be recorded.

Decorum in debate is always important, especially in a large meeting. It is discourteous to stand while another speaker has the floor. When the chairperson has assigned the floor to a speaker, it is proper for all others to be seated. As soon as that speaker finishes, another who wishes to speak should again stand and address the chair. The wise chairperson will be attentive to the various individuals who wish to speak and give each one a turn. The debater who is patient gains the respect of other members and adds weight to what he or she will eventually say. If, on the other hand, a debater shows disgust for the chair each time the floor is assigned to another, that person loses credibility when he or she finally gets to speak.

A basic principle of decorum in debate is that motions are debated, personalities are not. The decorous speaker will always avoid any reference of any kind to the individual who made the motion. Discussion is limited to the merits of the motion, not the merit or lack of merit of the maker of the motion. Those in leadership in church groups must help all to understand that a strong feeling against a certain proposal does not carry with it a feeling against the person who proposed it. If a speaker does verbally attack any individual in the group, it is the duty of the chair to stop the speaker and rule him or her out of order. Then if that person does not cease the verbal attacks, he or she can be ordered out of the assembly. If the chair fails to halt such a speaker, anyone else in the assembly can interrupt the speaker, calling for a point of order.

Proper decorum in debate adds greatly to the speakers' leadership ability. If speakers realize their speech is becoming too heated and know that they are about to lose their self-control, they should pause until they can speak in normal conversational manner. It is a psychological fact that the second speaker will respond to the first speaker's tone of voice. Those who are so convinced of the correctness of their propositions that they can speak slowly and with deliberate conviction convey the confidence that usually carries the issue. Those who are so uncertain of their facts that they must resort to loudness, indecorum, and attack quite artlessly reveal their uncertainty.

In conventions and assemblies one individual may want to speak several times on the same motion. A common rule of order is that no one can speak more than twice on a motion if anyone objects. If there is such an objection, a motion to suspend the rules to allow the person to speak again would be in order. This motion would require a two-thirds vote to carry. Of course, if there are no objections, a person can speak repeatedly on the same motion.

There will be times in large conventions or assemblies when the *division of the assembly, division of the vote*, or *division* will be requested. This is a demand, and as such it can interrupt a speaker. It requires no second, is not debatable, and cannot be amended. It relates only to voice votes. Such a demand is made when someone feels that the voice vote (Ayes and Noes) sounded about the same, and doubts the ruling of the chair. When the chair hears the outcry "Division" in any of its forms, he or she immediately says, "A division of the vote has been called for. All in favor of the motion will rise. Be seated. All opposed to the motion will rise. Be seated. The affirmative (negative) has it, and the motion is carried (lost)." The assembly should always be prepared to have someone help with the counting, and it should be made clear that only registered delegates are to vote.

Whenever a voice vote sounds close, it is wise for the presiding officer to say, "The chair believes the Ayes (Noes) have it." Then he or she pauses for a second or two before continuing, "The Ayes (Noes) do have it, and the motion is carried (lost)." This procedure allows time for anyone to demand division, but more importantly, it impressively demonstrates the complete fairness of the chair.

Most large group meetings should have the services of a recognized *parliamentarian*. The American Institute of Parliamentarians, 203 West Wayne, Suite 312, Fort Wayne, Indiana, 46802, will provide a list of qualified experts. The fees they charge are reasonable and well worth the extra expense to a large organization.

At a convention or assembly meeting, the parliamentarian should not serve in this responsible position without a conference with the presiding officer before the meeting. This conference should enable the parliamentarian to give whatever instruction the presiding officer requests. The presiding officer must feel capable of conducting the meeting properly and expeditiously. The parliamentarian sometimes prepares a small card on which is written the proper wording for putting a matter to a vote, as well as the proper wording for using general consent. The parliamentarian is also available to any committee to instruct its chairperson in the most helpful way to present the committee's report.

In the meeting the parliamentarian usually sits near the presiding officer. The presiding officer can call upon the parliamentarian at any time, except when someone is speaking or during voting, to give an opinion on the parliamentary status of that which is before the assembly. Such advice or information from the parliamentarian is not binding on the presiding officer, who always retains the right to rule according to his or her own judgment. The ultimate authority lies with the assembly. If it disagrees with the ruling of the chair, the assembly can appeal the ruling.

The assembly has the right to ask the advice of the parliamentarian; any member may do so by gaining the floor on a point of order and stating this request. The chair then asks the parliamentarian to advise the group on the parliamentary situation. Again, the chair is not obligated to follow the advice of the parliamentarian. If a member appeals the ruling of the chair, the assembly can either sustain or reject the ruling by voting on it. The ultimate authority in a business session lies with the group as it follows its own bylaws, not with the chairperson or the parliamentarian.

Handling Resolutions

One of the most frustrating convention experiences is sitting through a convention meeting during the debate on and adoption of resolutions. The tendency to use improper parliamentary procedure in this area is most prevalent. The following steps are suggested as the correct and expeditious manner of handling resolutions at a state or national convention or assembly.

The chairperson of the resolutions committee presents a first reading of the committee report at the appointed time on the agenda. If action is to be taken later, the presiding officer thanks the chairperson of the committee and announces the time when action will take place. In this case no motions of any kind should be made following this first reading of the committee's report. As is the case with all reports, the committee's report is received by hearing it read. Consequently, the motion that the report be received would be out of order because the assembly has already received it. A motion to *adopt the report* would be the formal action of passing the resolutions as they have been presented, right on the spot.

The only time the motion to *receive a report* is in order is before the report has been presented and there is some objection to having it given at the time specified for it on the agenda. The reason for such an objection may be that the report should be held up until a particular key person arrives. In the event of objection, someone else could move, "That we receive the report," meaning "Let's hear it now!" Such a motion needs a second, is debatable, and amendable, and requires a majority vote.

When the time comes for action to be taken on the resolutions, the best procedure is to have the report photocopied in advance and distributed in the meeting to all the delegates. The presiding officer calls for the chairperson of the resolutions committee to come to the front. The committee chairperson says to the presiding officer, "Mr. or Madam Chairperson, our committee would like to suggest that we take action on the resolutions one natural section at a time." The presiding officer, standing at his or her desk or table, states to the body, "If there are no objections, we will take action on the resolutions one natural section at a time. Are there any objections? Hearing none, the chair rules that we will take action on the resolutions one natural section at a time." Here again is the wise use of the general consent technique.

After agreement to take action on the report one natural section at a time, moving to adopt all of the resolutions except the ones that are obviously going to be debated is out of order. The chairperson will remind the members that the resolutions are to be considered one natural section at a time. The resolutions usually cover a multitude of subjects. They can be confusing and disturbing to the delegates if the delegates lose the sequence of what is being discussed.

For the actual consideration of the sections, the presiding officer turns to the chairperson of the resolutions committee, indicating that he or she is to step forward. The chairperson then addresses the presiding officer, "Section One, Mr. or Madam Chairman; I move the adoption of Section One." Only the number of the section is given; the first reading of the report to the group makes a second verbatim reading unnecessary. The presiding officer states: "It is moved that we adopt Section One. Is there discussion?" (No committee report ever needs a second.) If there should be discussion or amendments or other kinds of allowable motions, such as to substitute or post-

pone, they are to be handled by the procedures
normally used for discussing or amending main
motions. The members are free to do whatever
they wish with any of the resolutions placed before them.

In such a large assembly or convention, a
delegate who wishes to speak to the resolution
should gain the floor by rising, addressing the
chair, and gaining recognition. It would be helpful
if the delegate explains, "I rise to speak in favor
of (against) the resolution . . ." or closes his or her
remarks with the words "Therefore, I urge the
defeat (acceptance) of the resolution." Such
phrasing will make clear to the listeners just
what the position of the speaker is in regard to
that particular resolution.

Occasionally there may be a rare person who
is neither for nor against the resolution but who
has pertinent information that would be helpful.
Upon gaining the floor, he or she may begin by
saying, "Mr. or Madam Chairperson, I rise to
speak neither in favor of the resolution nor
against it. I do, however, have some information
that might help the group as they search for a
consensus." For example, this person may be able
to report on the status of legislation in Congress
relating to the subject of this particular resolution.

When the presiding officer feels that discussion is over on the particular section under consideration, he or she says, "Hearing no further discussion, all in favor of adopting Section One will say 'Aye.' Those opposed will say 'No.' The Ayes (Noes) have it, and Section One is adopted (lost) ."

Then the chairperson of the resolutions committee again steps forward and moves the adoption of Section Two of the committee report. The presiding officer states the motion and again calls for discussion. This procedure is followed through all of the sections of the resolutions, thereby offering full latitude for any debate, amending, deleting, or substituting procedures. When the last resolution has been adopted, no motion of any kind is required. This method of dealing with resolutions is uncluttered and will help any group avoid needless delay.

Resolutions can be submitted from the floor, in writing, without coming through the resolutions committee, unless otherwise specified in the bylaws. Sometimes a person who has submitted a resolution to the resolutions committee but does not hear it read in the committee's report is nonetheless anxious to have it come before the assembly. If the bylaws do not provide otherwise, that person can offer an amendment or a substitute to any pending section when it is being considered. Or, following the disposition of the last of

the committee's resolutions, the person may offer
the resolution from the floor, first presenting it
in writing to the clerk. Then the person moves
the resolution. This motion requires a second, is
debatable, is amendable, and requires a majority
vote to carry. This provision fulfills one of the
basic principles of parliamentary law: "The minority must be heard."[13]

In conventions or large assemblies a *formal
resolution* is sometimes proposed. This should not
be confused with the resolutions offered by the
resolutions committee. It also differs from a simple motion in that it is much more formal in
construction. It could have a preamble in which
a sentiment is set forth, a few "whereas" statements, and then the wording "Therefore, be it
resolved that . . ." The entire wording of such a
formal resolution based on sentiment and feeling
should be worked out in detail before it is presented, in order to avoid unnecessary amending
procedures. Amending procedures would not be
out of order, but they weaken such a resolution.
The proposed resolution should be so strong and
should reflect such considered judgment that it
does not need amending. If the proposition has
not had this much attention, then it should be
proposed as a simple main motion.

In a state or national convention or assembly,
resolutions should either be eliminated from the

agenda entirely or have ample time programmed to provide for full discussion and responsible action.

The presiding officer cannot arbitrarily limit the time for debating the resolutions, nor can he or she arbitrarily change the agenda to accommodate discussion of the resolutions. The presiding officer does not have the right to make such a ruling on his or her own authority. In every business meeting of every church group an educational process is going on. The process is teaching either good or bad group decision-making procedures. If the presiding officer arbitrarily rules on the time of debate, the worst kind of procedure is being demonstrated. No one can impinge upon the rights of the group without the affirmative two-thirds vote of that group!

If time slips away (often the fault of the presiding officer for not adhering to the order of the day, i.e., the agenda), the presiding officer can say properly, "If there are no objections, we will limit the debate on the resolutions to thirty minutes. Are there any objections? Hearing none, the chair rules that debate on the resolutions will be limited to thirty minutes." If this action of general consent fails because there are objections, then a motion, second, and two-thirds vote would be needed to limit debate. This procedure can be used to limit the debate as a whole or to limit each speaker. If necessary, the limits can be changed by a second motion, handled in the same way as the initial motion to limit debate. The same procedure of general consent or a formal motion can be used to change the agenda to allow additional time for resolutions at another point in the program, if this seems desirable to all concerned. In this way, the rights of the group are always protected.

In summary, the correct business meeting procedure is the easiest business meeting procedure.

Notes

13. Grumme, *Parliamentary Law and Protocol*, 7.

Bibliography

Demeter, George. *Demeter's Manual of Parliamentary Law and Procedure*. Boston: Bostonia Press, 1961.

Grumme, Marguerite. *Basic Principles of Parliamentary Law and Protocol*. Westwood, New Jersey: Fleming H. Revell Co., 1963.

Jones, O. Garfield. *Parliamentary Procedure at a Glance*. New York: The Meredith Publishing Co., 1949.

Robert, Henry M. *Robert's Rules of Order*. rev. ed., Old Tappan, New Jersey: Fleming H. Revell Co., 1980.

Sturgis, Alice F. *Sturgis' Standard Code of Parliamentary Procedure*. New York: McGraw-Hill Book Co., 1966.

Index

accept, adopt, approve, 47, 104

addressing the chair, 32–35, 98–99

adjournment, 56–57, 96

agenda, 58, 96–98, 109

amend, 58, 61–62

amendments,

    method of making, 49–54

    role of, 49

    third degree, 52

appeal from the decision of the chair, 63–64

assigning the floor, 33

ballot

    cast by clerk, 76–78

    voting by, 76–79

    See also Voting

bylaws, 82–83, 84

    amending of, 42

    cannot be suspended, 46

call for order of the day, 56, 58, 97

call for previous question. *See* Previous Question, Meaning and Rules of

call of a pastor, 30–32

chair. *See* Presiding Officer

consider paragraph by

paragraph. *See* Divide
the Motion or Question

commit (refer) to a committee or board, 58, 61, 85

committee of the whole, 29

committees, 81–94

freedom for discussion in,
22, 28–29, 83–84

general, 81–94

nominating, 12, 74–75,
79–80

pastor's influence on,
10–12, 87–90, 93–94

reports, 45, 46

resolutions, 103–5

rules for, 83–84

special, 84–86

consider the matter, 29

debate

decorum in, 28, 40, 98–100

extend (or limit), 58, 60

number of times a
member may speak and
time allowed, 37, 60, 64, 100

rules concerning, 34–35,
64–65, 109–10

determined will, 8–9

disagreement, 8–10

divide the motion or question, 62–63

division of the assembly
(division of the vote or
division), 100–101

elections, 73–80

certification of, 73

closing of nominations,
63, 75–77

nominating committee,
74–75

nominations from the floor,
74, 75

voting, 75–79

when officers assume
positions, 80

See also Voting

ex officio member, rights
and privileges, 87, 88,
89

filling the blanks, 65–67

floor, obtaining of. *See* Addressing the Chair

formal resolution, 108

general consent, 22, 38–39,
57, 58, 64, 65, 75, 84,
86, 96

germane, as it applies to amendments, 51

informal consideration (without a motion), 28–29

leadership, how to develop parliamentary, 81, 88–94

minority report from a committee, 86–87

moderator. *See* Presiding Officer

motion, motions

commonly misused, 24–32

declared carried or lost, 23, 36–37

duty of chairperson with respect to, 16, 17, 19, 25, 26, 27, 37

duty of secretary with respect to, 36

incidental, 56, 62–67

making, 25

modifying, 39

postponing, 26–28, 59

privileged, 55, 56–58, 96, 97

rank of, 55–56

responsibility of the maker of, 25, 37

restoratory, 56, 67–72

result of committee report, 47

speaking to, 19, 37–38, 100

stating, 19, 22–23

subsidiary, 55, 58–62

substitute, 52–54, 86–87

tabling, 25–26, 58–59, 96 *See also* Table

to consider a matter, 29

to refer, 85

voting on, 23

withdrawing, 37–38, 64

See also Seconding Motions

nominations, 73–80

closing, 63, 75, 76–77

committee's report, 74–75, 79–80

reopening, 63

objection to consideration, 28

parliamentarian, importance and role of, 101–2

parliamentary procedure

definition of, 7

importance of, 12–13

principles of, 7, 32–33

pastor

as ex officio board member, 88–89

role of in business meetings, 10–12

permissive will, 8–9

point of order, 46, 63, 99, 102

postponement

indefinite, 27–28, 58, 62

to a definite time, 26, 58, 59, 60–61

See also Table

presiding officer,

character qualities of, 20–22

declaring meeting adjourned, 57

declaring motion carried or lost, 19, 23, 101

declaring officers elected, 76, 77

pastor serving as, 21
See also Pastor

restating a motion, 23

restrictions on, 16–18

role of, 15–24

speaking in defense of a ruling, 64

speaking to a motion, 17

stating a motion, 16, 19, 22–23, 25, 26, 36

voting privileges of, 23–24, 78

wise use of general consent, 22, 38–39

previous question, meaning and rules of, 33–35, 59

priorities for boards and committees, 90–92

question of privilege, 33–35, 56, 57

question, calling for, always discourteous and wrong, 33–35

quorum, 88

assumption of, 42

business allowable in absence of, 42–43

ratification of action taken in absence of, 43

significance of, 41

ratify, 67, 71

recess, 56, 57

reconsider and enter, 69, 70

reconsideration of a motion, 67, 68–69, 70

reconsideration of a vote, 29–30

refer. *See* Commit (Refer) to a Committee or Board

reports,

presentation of, 16

rules for adopting, accepting, approving, receiving, 47, 104

rescind (repeal), 67, 69–70

resignations, 47

resolutions, 103–10

at state and national meetings, 103, 108–9

from the floor, 107–8

rules of order, 67

seconding motions, 68, 69, 70

importance and meaning of, 47

unnecessary for committee reports, 47

unnecessary to get name of seconder, 47, 98

withdraw if motion is modified, 39

session, difference between meeting and, 95–96

special meetings, 45–46

standing and sitting, 19–20

suspending the rules, 67

table, 58

most abused motion, 25–28

take from the, 67, 72, 96

tellers, responsibilities of, 78–79

tie votes, chair's vote, 23 *See also* Voting

treasurer's report, 46

unanimous consent. *See* General Consent

unfinished business, 45

voting

ballot for, 65

chair's right of, 23–24

choosing a method of, 65

correct manner of, 23

duty of chair to announce
    result of, 23, 36

lot, 79

majority vote, 6, 7, 26, 27,
    31, 50, 57, 61, 64, 65, 68,
    71, 77, 104, 108

on new members, 43–44

rising (standing) to vote,
    26, 65, 77, 101

two-thirds vote, 24, 26,
    28, 31–32, 34, 37, 59, 60,
    61, 67, 70, 75, 76, 77, 97,
    98, 100

unanimous vote, 29, 30,
    31, 84

voice vote, 65, 78, 100

when chair is doubted,
    101

when "division" is called,
    100–101

when no one votes, 24

You Can Acquire in 20 Minutes a 50% Basic Knowledge of Parliamentary Law

Study this page for 10 minutes. Repeat out loud.

Say; "There are three classes of motions: Privileged, Subsidiary and Principal. The obvious symbols S,D,A,M,R enable me to learn their rules at once: S means the motion needs a Second, D it is Debatable, A Amendable, M means Majority vote, R it can be Reconsidered. (Repeat it.) I must now learn their rank; this means, when any one of them is before the body (pick any one) it is in order to propose any motion(s) listed above it in rank, but not any listed below it; just like auction bids on an Article. (Repeat.) Now, as the Subsidiary motions are used often at meetings I can easily learn their order to rank from their first letter L,PL,PR,A,P (L for Lay on table, P for Previous question, L for Limit debate, P for Postpone," etc.)

(Permission is given to adopt or quote from this page for your organization's purposes.)

THREE CLASSES OF MOTIONS HERE

I. The Privileged (only 5)

1. Fix a time at which to adjourn (S,A,M,R)
2. Adjourn (S,M)
3. Recess (S,A,M)
4. Raise a question of privilege (no symbols)
5. Call for the orders of the day (no symbols)

II. The Subsidiary (just 7)

1. Lay on the table (S,M)
2. Previous question (S,R,2/3)
3. Limit debate, or extend it (S,A,R,2/3)
4. Postpone to a definite time (S,D,A,M,R)
5. Refer, or commit: or re-commit (S,D,A,M,R)
6. Amend (S,D,A,M,R)
7. Postpone Indefinitely (S,D,M,R)

III. The Principal (one at a time)

1. Main Motion; or Resolution (S,D,A,M,R)

Quiz: Give the basic rules of a Main Motion; Resolution; Refer, Table; Adjourn. What mean the symbols S,D,A,M,R? Which motions need 2/3 vote? Name the 7 Subsidiary Motions. (Master this page at once.)

Used by permission of Atty. George Demeter, Parliamentarian. Astor Box 275, Boston, Massachusetts 02123.